SUE HACKMAN

# Hodder Reading Project
**Teacher's Resource**

**LEVEL 2–3**

# Hodder Murray
A MEMBER OF THE HODDER HEADLINE GROUP

*The Publishers would like to thank the following for permission to reproduce copyright material:*
**Copyright photos**
p.15 Tarantula © Bruce Coleman Inc./Alamy; p.39 Cobra © John Terence Turner/Alamy; p.40 Snake Charmer © Michael Fairchild/Still Pictures; p.67 Martin Luther King © Flip Schulke/Corbis.

**Copyright artwork**
pp.2, 52, 53, 54, 55, 71, 72, 73, 77, 78 and 79 © Gary Andrews; pp.16, 17, 39, 59, 65 and 94 © Barking Dog; p.85 © Oxford Designers and Illustrators.

*Every effort has been made to trace all copyright holders, but if any have been inadvertently overlooked the Publishers will be pleased to make the necessary arrangements at the first opportunity.*

Although every effort has been made to ensure that website addresses are correct at time of going to press, Hodder Murray cannot be responsible for the content of any website mentioned in this book. It is sometimes possible to find a relocated web page by typing in the address of the home page for a website in the URL window of your browser.

Hodder Headline's policy is to use papers that are natural, renewable and recyclable products and made from wood grown in sustainable forests. The logging and manufacturing processes are expected to conform to the environmental regulations of the country of origin.

Orders: please contact Bookpoint Ltd, 130 Milton Park, Abingdon, Oxon OX14 4SB. Telephone: (44) 01235 827720. Fax: (44) 01235 400454. Lines are open from 9.00am to 6.00pm, Monday to Saturday, with a 24-hour message answering service. Visit our website at www.hoddereducation.co.uk

© Sue Hackman 2006
First published in 2006 by
Hodder Murray, an imprint of Hodder Education,
a member of the Hodder Headline Group
338 Euston Road
London NW1 3BH

Impression number    10 9 8 7 6 5 4 3
Year                 2011 2010 2009 2008 2007 2006 (three times)

All rights reserved. Apart from any use permitted under UK copyright law, no part of this publication may be reproduced or transmitted in any form or by any means, electronic or mechanical, including photocopying and recording, or held within any information storage and retrieval system, without permission in writing from the publisher or under licence from the Copyright Licensing Agency Limited. Further details of such licences (for reprographic reproduction) may be obtained from the Copyright Licensing Agency Limited, 90 Tottenham Court Road, London W1T 4LP.

Cover photo: Balloons © Royalty-Free/Corbis.
Typeset by DC Graphic Design Limited, Swanley, Kent.
Printed in Great Britain by Hobbs the Printers, Totton, Hants.

A catalogue record for this title is available from the British Library

ISBN-10:  0 340 88355 3
ISBN-13:  9 780 340 88355 6

# CONTENTS

## Using the scheme — 1
Aims of the scheme — 1
Scheme contents — 1
How the scheme works — 2
About the Pupil's Book — 3
About the reading books — 4
About assessment — 4
About the Teacher's Resource — 4

## What is involved in moving from Level 2 to Level 3 in reading? — 5
Securing progress through Level 2 — 5
Progressing to Level 3 — 6
The language used in the Pupil's Book and reading books — 9

## STEP 1: Assess what your pupils can already do — 10
Test 1: The Wood — 11
Test 2: Tarantula — 15
Class Record of Progress — 19
Pupil Record of Progress — 20

## STEP 2: Set personal reading targets for Level 2–3 readers — 21
Target cards — 22

## STEP 3: Use the Pupil's Book to teach and to track progress — 23
Teaching plans for the Pupil's Book — 24
A: The Reading Experience — 24
B: Responding to Reading — 25
C: Reading Strategies — 26
D: Finding What You Need — 27
E: Literature — 28

## STEP 4: Use the reading books to apply and consolidate learning — 29
Matching Level 2 texts to skills and strategies — 30
Matching Level 3 texts to skills and strategies — 31
Introducing the books to groups — 32

## STEP 5: Reassess pupils at the end of the scheme    34
    Test 3: The Barn    35
    Test 4: Cobra    39

## Information about the reading books, including photocopy masters: Level 2    44

  1  The Underground    44
  2  Shop Till You Drop    49
  3  Ant & Dec    56
  4  Martin Luther King    62
  5  Place Your Bets    68
  6  I Never Done Nothing    74

## Information about the reading books, including photocopy masters: Level 3    81

  7  Foul Play    81
  8  Urban Myths    86
  9  The Black Death    90
10  You won't believe this but…    95
11  Mini-sagas    98
12  The Red Fox    101

# Using the scheme

## Aims of the scheme

The *Hodder Reading Project* is a series of textbooks for improving the reading of secondary-age pupils at National Curriculum Levels 2–3, 3–4, 4–5 and 5–6. Each Pupil's Book is supported by reading books in which pupils apply, consolidate and practise their new skills. A Teacher's Resource including guidance, teaching plans and pupil reading instructions accompanies each set of materials.

This particular set of materials is targeted at pupils who have secured Level 2 and are progressing on to Level 3. It contains a Pupil's Book, a Teacher's Resource and 12 reading books.

## Scheme contents

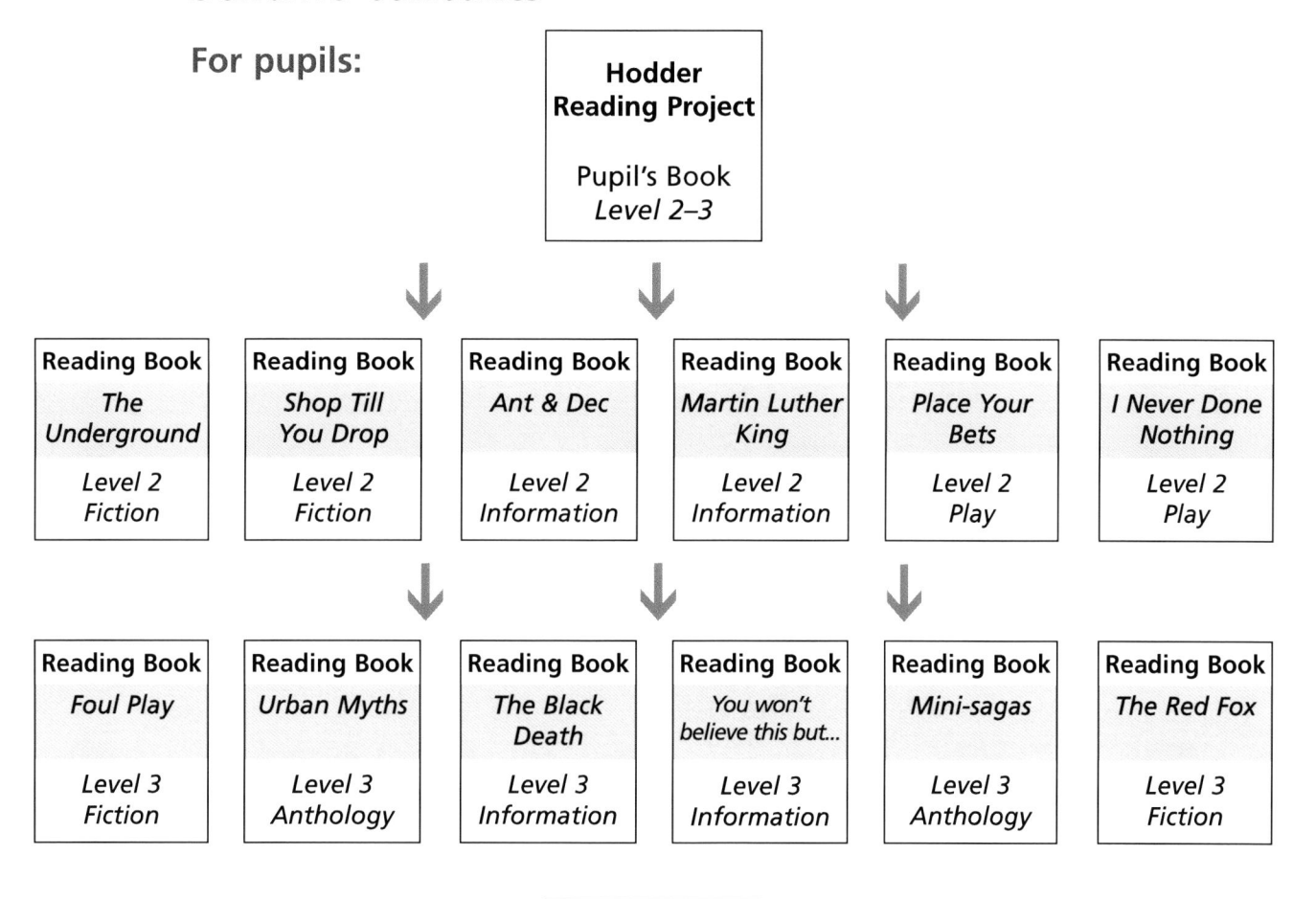

For pupils:

**Hodder Reading Project**
Pupil's Book
Level 2–3

| Reading Book | Reading Book | Reading Book | Reading Book | Reading Book | Reading Book |
|---|---|---|---|---|---|
| *The Underground* | *Shop Till You Drop* | *Ant & Dec* | *Martin Luther King* | *Place Your Bets* | *I Never Done Nothing* |
| Level 2 Fiction | Level 2 Fiction | Level 2 Information | Level 2 Information | Level 2 Play | Level 2 Play |

| Reading Book | Reading Book | Reading Book | Reading Book | Reading Book | Reading Book |
|---|---|---|---|---|---|
| *Foul Play* | *Urban Myths* | *The Black Death* | *You won't believe this but...* | *Mini-sagas* | *The Red Fox* |
| Level 3 Fiction | Level 3 Anthology | Level 3 Information | Level 3 Information | Level 3 Anthology | Level 3 Fiction |

For teachers:

**Hodder Reading Project**
Teacher's Resource
Level 2–3

# HRP Teacher's Resource: Level 2 → 3

The *Hodder Reading Project: Level 2–3* is designed to support pupils with reading ages considerably below their chronological ages. It provides appropriate content and allows the maximum possible independence of the reader. The Pupil's Book is written so that most pupils can use it alone, but ideally supported by a teacher who leads them through the key ideas. It is anticipated that the reading books will be tackled by pupils organised in groups for mutual support, but can also be used independently by the pupil or supported by a helpful adult.

## How the scheme works

**STEP 1** Informal reading Tests 1 and 2 may be used to evaluate pupils' reading profile

**STEP 2** Pupils' reading targets are set

**STEP 3** Teacher leads pupils through Pupil's Book to teach and track progress

**STEP 4** Pupils apply new skills in reading groups using the reading books to consolidate learning

**STEP 5** Pupils may be retested using informal reading Tests 3 and 4

# About the Pupil's Book

The Pupil's Book contains 15 masterclasses, which focus on the skills and strategies of reading:

**A The Reading Experience**
Masterclass 1: Seeing what you read
Masterclass 2: What next?
Masterclass 3: Feeling it

**B Responding to Reading**
Masterclass 4: Using your experience
Masterclass 5: Thinking aloud
Masterclass 6: Reading like a detective

**C Reading Strategies**
Masterclass 7: Sounding out words you don't know
Masterclass 8: Working out words you don't know
Masterclass 9: Reading longer sentences

**D Finding What You Need**
Masterclass 10: Finding information
Masterclass 11: Seeing what's there
Masterclass 12: Making notes

**E Literature**
Masterclass 13: Choosing a novel
Masterclass 14: Writing a book review
Masterclass 15: Answering test questions

Each masterclass is six pages long and concludes with an assessment task. Criteria are provided for these assessment tasks so that pupils can understand what is credited. It also allows them to self-mark or peer-mark.

It is envisaged that teachers will first use the Pupil's Book to introduce all the reading skills, using the assessment task to determine the level of success of individual pupils in each masterclass. The profile of success will be used to determine which reading books are prioritised for which pupils. This way, pupils are challenged to use and consolidate the skills they have acquired from the Pupil's Book.

**HRP Teacher's Resource: Level 2 → 3**

## About the reading books

There are 12 reading books at this level of the scheme, of which six are suitable for Level 2 readers and six are suitable for Level 3 readers. In each set of six, there are two fiction books, two information books and two 'other' drawn from a range of texts such as plays and puzzles.

Each set of six books is chosen to practise all the skills and strategies taught in the Pupil's Book. These are introduced to you on pages 30–31, so that you can see where the opportunities lie to address each skill.

It is envisaged that pupils will be organised in small groups to read together, stopping occasionally to discuss what they are reading and to undertake activities.

Each book is supported by a sheet of instructions. This guides pupils through the book and sets questions and activities at certain staging points. These sheets are offered as photocopy masters within this Teacher's Resource.

## About assessment

There are several opportunities to assess pupil progress:

1. Tests 1 and 2 at the start of the scheme. These tests indicate which masterclasses are most needed. Pupil targets are allocated on the basis of the results.
2. Assessment tasks at the end of each masterclass in the Pupil's Book.
3. Tests 3 and 4 at the end of the scheme. These tests indicate where progress has been made and where attention is still required.

## About the Teacher's Resource

This book contains guidance about using the scheme, and photocopy masters for the pupils.

# What is involved in moving from Level 2 to Level 3 in reading?

## → Securing progress through Level 2

Level 2 covers an unusually wide range of achievement.

→ In **the lower reaches of Level 2** there are readers who are at a very early stage of competence, using only partial clues and cues to make meaning. Their grasp of phonics may well be basic and incomplete. In particular, they may struggle with digraphs such as 'ie', 'ou' and 'ph'. They still have to work at the mechanics of reading, particularly with unknown texts, and tend to rely heavily on their memories, their sight vocabularies and easy phonics, where letters and sounds are closely related. They like familiar books and repetition because this gives them the sensation of fluency. They are much less secure when they work on an unfamiliar text, when they have to move word by word and contextual cues are not enough to compensate for poor phonics. They work best when they have support on hand to nudge them to choose and use an appropriate strategy. They nearly always read aloud to give voice to this decoding process.

→ Readers in **the middle range of Level 2** have realised that there are various strategies which can be used to get at the meaning of text. When they get stuck, they are able to attempt their own solutions, using phonics, backed by context and sight vocabulary, though many still lean heavily on a favourite method. This process may be slow, but it allows readers to tackle unknown words and unfamiliar texts. Readers at this level know how the reading ought to sound, and so they strive for fluency, but this usually comes in short runs, when they recognise familiar phrases and repetitions. They can deal with words which are phonically regular and well signalled by the context. There is a stop-and-start feel about the reading which is not unlike the early stages of learning a musical instrument. Mostly, pupils at this level read aloud, and if they try to read silently you will see their lips moving. They are reading aloud in their heads.

→ At **the upper reaches of Level 2** are readers who are trying to bring together the range of strategies that allow them to read simple books quite independently. Their purchase on phonics is more secure, and they have an increasing sense of which strategy will work best when they get stuck. Sometimes they pause to look ahead and see where they are going; sometimes they look at context and guess at a word (not always correctly); sometimes they do a full sound-by-sound breakdown. Their sight vocabulary is more confident. Impatient sometimes, they leap over obstacles by guessing and filling in, gaining fluency at the expense of accuracy. More anxious readers at this level do the opposite, plumping for accuracy at the expense of fluency. But they do feel like readers; they have attained a measure of independence which grows as they build their experience and their confidence. They internalise the reading voice when they are reading – or rereading – simple books.

The National Curriculum attainment target for reading defines Level 2 in these terms:

> **Level 2**
> Pupils' reading of simple texts shows understanding and is generally accurate. They express opinions about major events or ideas in stories, poems and non-fiction. They use more than one strategy, such as phonic, graphic, syntactic and contextual, in reading unfamiliar words and establishing meaning.

Pupils' appreciation of literature at Level 2 is well ahead of their reading capability, and this is particularly true of the older reader. A typical secondary pupil working at Level 2 will have had years to hear, follow and enjoy stories and will know what to expect. Older pupils are familiar with popular genres such as science fiction, thriller, romance, fantasy and detective genres, stock storylines and characters. Much of this is drawn from anecdote, listening to stories and watching television and films. The older reader has the advantage of being able to draw on a wide hinterland of narrative experience.

It is in non-fiction where this hinterland is more restricted. Non-fiction texts are less predictable and formulaic; they lack the repetition and patterns of language that offer such useful support in reading fiction. More positively, many boys at this level are motivated by non-fiction because it releases them from the empathetic processes of narrative, which they see as 'girly'. Factual photographs feel more comfortable than fictional illustrations (which are reminiscent of infant reading schemes).

To summarise, the progress of pupils over Level 2 is principally about mobilising a repertoire of strategies to get at meaning and to build confidence and fluency.

## Progressing to Level 3

If Level 2 pupils are discovering a range of strategies for reading, then Level 3 pupils are deploying them smartly. Level 3 pupils orchestrate a range of strategies to fix the meaning of the text and, because they are more fluent, they have an increasing capacity for self-checking and accuracy. The mechanics of reading are coming under control so that, for simple texts, they can spend more of their mental energies responding to the meaning and engaging in imaginative participation.

Level 2 is not without imaginative involvement, of course. Pupils at every level are stimulated by intriguing storylines, struck by pictures and responsive to the patterns of language. Indeed, when Level 2 readers *hear* fiction, this response is very clear. But when they try to read independently, the force of the themes, language and events is limited by the pace of decoding. It is a very frustrating phase of development for the reader. Level 3 readers, by contrast, have acquired sufficient skill to process text with relative fluency, and as long as the text does not trip them up too often on complex vocabulary and taxing sentence structures, they have spare mental capacity to devote to imaginative response.

# Progressing to Level 3

Imaginative participation is core to the development of Level 3 readers. They interact with the text, animating the words in their minds so that they create a virtual world in which the events or information are played out. They are active readers who see images as they read; they ask questions ("Why is she doing that?" "What's going on here?" "What will happen next?"); they make judgements; they compare it against their own experiences; they empathise and sympathise; they reread and revise their opinions. The reader at the end of Level 3 is undergoing a mental rehearsal of the text. And over time it becomes fuller and more sophisticated.

Glancing ahead briefly to Level 4, we see the same reader beginning to project beyond the text. Not only does he or she imagine its content and events, but the reader begins to read between the lines, using inference and deduction to fill out its implied and hidden meanings. Even further along the line, he or she recognises the text as something created, an artefact created by a writer which is comparable with others.

Level 3 readers are still grappling with the mechanics of reading, of course, but have a basic repertoire of phonics, sight vocabulary, reading experience, skills and strategies to support them. Much of their success in reading depends on their ability to increase this repertoire and make it work for more complex texts. Crucially they need to push beyond the familiar letters and sounds to the less common versions such as 'augh' and 'ough' and the ones that can have different enunciations such as 'ow' and 'our'. They also encounter longer and more irregular words, and more complex sentences. They must learn to choose the most efficient strategy for cracking a new word or guessing at its meaning. They must also learn to scan ahead to see the structure of a longer sentence.

The National Curriculum attainment target defines Level 3 reading in the following terms:

> **Level 3**
> Pupils read a range of texts fluently and accurately. They read independently, using strategies appropriately to establish meaning. In responding to fiction and non-fiction they show understanding of the main points and express preferences. They use their knowledge of the alphabet to locate books and find information.

One of the main reasons why pupils get stuck at this level is that teachers leave off teaching them because they have attained a certain amount of independence in their reading. For some pupils, even in Key Stage 1, this does work. They generalise from their experience and thoughtful provision of texts leads them in careful steps to the next stage. But it is reasonably safe to assume that if they reach secondary schools still at Level 3 this method has already failed. Something more is needed. It is teaching. This does not mean abandoning independent reading; rather, it means doing both. That is what this scheme attempts to do: to combine teaching with texts.

**HRP Teacher's Resource: Level 2 → 3**

This part of the reading scheme addresses the progress of pupils to mid-Level 3, and the upper levels of it are addressed in the next book in the series, *Hodder Reading Project: Level 3–4.* By the midway point, the aim is to have shifted pupils' reading 'horizon' from the end of the sentence to the end of the paragraph, as they begin to pull away from word and sentence level considerations to attend to paragraphs, chapters and whole texts. For pupils, the process of reading should feel increasingly natural, and certainly there will be times when they feel truly independent readers.

To summarise, the progress of pupils over Level 3 is principally about developing their imaginative response to texts, and securing their confidence in tackling longer and more complex reading texts.

## The language used in the Pupil's Book and reading books

The language specification for the Pupil's Book and reading books assumes that:

- Pupils know letter sounds
- Pupils know the common consonant digraphs (one sound made with two letters, such as 'sh', 'th', 'ch')
- Pupils know the most common vowel digraphs (such as 'ow', 'ai', 'oo')
- Pupils are able to blend letter sounds which are regular and predictable
- Pupils have a sight vocabulary of the most common everyday words (such as *because, once, people* or *police*)

Words that are trickier than this are only introduced if they are well supported by the context so that they have cues to work them out. Indeed, it is important that a reading scheme at this level provides some challenges to work on.

There are some specific places where longer and less regular words have been introduced specifically to follow up masterclasses C7: Sounding out words you don't know, and C8: Working out words you don't know, but these are signalled in the objectives column and are the explicit subject of questions in the **Reading instructions**. They can all be 'cracked' using sounding-out strategies, context and etymology.

# STEP 1
# Assess what your pupils can already do

You may wish, at the outset, to get a snapshot of achievement among your pupils. Two simple tests can be found on pages 11–12 and 15–16. These will help you to estimate how well developed your pupils' skills are in the five areas covered by the Pupil's Book. They come in two photocopiable papers (Test 1 and Test 2), for which you should allow approximately 30 minutes each in conditions as close as possible to timed silence, without causing unnecessary tension. The tests can be set in two different lessons. Timing is less important than finishing the paper, as you need to know what pupils can do.

It is acceptable to read questions aloud, but not the text itself. Likewise, you can clarify what questions are looking for without telling the pupils how to go about answering.

Test 1 covers Sections A, B and C of the Pupil's Book. Test 2 covers sections D and E.

The mark schemes can be found on pages 13–14 and 17–18.

If you wish to record progress, then fill in the result for each section into the **Class Record of Progress**, which can be found on page 19.

# TEST 1

# The Wood

At the back of Gran's house was a wood. When Kay was on her swing, she could peep over the top of the fence and see the trees and a small white path that led into the forest. At first she was afraid, but soon she began to think of ways to get over the fence and go into the wood.

On the third day of her visit, a sudden whim took her over the fence   5
and she made her way to the small white path between the trees.

The wood was thick and dark and quiet. No birds sang. No small animals skittered in the leaves. The branches hung low. Kay shivered but she wanted to see more, and along the path she found it. Up ahead, she saw light and hurried towards it.   10

What Kay found was a clearing with grass. The sun shone down. In the clearing stood a huge tree. Kay knew it was an oak, but this oak was not like any oak that Kay had seen before. For one thing, it was full of birds and creepers with large flowers. The grass around the roots was trampled flat. Its branches were hung with many items: foil stars, bird trays,   15
wind chimes and bells. And there was a door.

Kay stood still. She knew what Gran would say. She knew what Dad would say. But she also knew her own heart, and she knew then what to do.

HRP Teacher's Resource: Level 2 → 3

## Questions

1 How does Kay feel as she walks into the wood, and what makes you think that?

2 Draw the oak tree.

3 What will Kay do next, and what makes you think that?

4 How can you explain the strange oak tree?

5 What *would* Kay's Gran and Dad say?

6 About how old is Kay, and how do you know?

7 What is a *sudden whim* (line 5)?

8 What does *skittered* mean (line 8)?

9 What is a *clearing* (line 11)?

10 What does the last sentence mean?

## Test 1: Mark scheme

### Question 1: How does Kay feel as she walks into the wood, and what makes you think that? (4 marks)

- 1 mark for recognising that she is slightly afraid
- Half a mark each for any two clues about the danger signalled in the darkness, the closeness and the silence of the wood
- 1 mark for recognising that she is driven by curiosity, impulse or maybe even boredom
- 1 mark for any reasoning to back up this part of the answer

### Question 2: Draw the oak tree. (4 marks)

- Ignore poor graphic skills; mark for content. Give half a mark each for:
  - birds
  - flowering creepers
  - trampled grass and roots at the base
  - foil stars
  - bird trays
  - wind chimes
  - bells
  - door

### Question 3: What will Kay do next, and what makes you think that? (2 marks)

- 1 mark for realising that Kay will approach the door and try to find out what is going on; 0 marks for saying she will leave it
- 1 mark for an attempt to justify this view; similar credit if any other view is rationalised

> Add up the marks out of 10 for Questions 1–3.
> This is the score for **Section A: The Reading Experience**.

### Question 4: How can you explain the strange oak tree? (4 marks)

- 1 mark for one reasonable answer, e.g. fairy dwelling
- 1 mark for any alternative answer, e.g. playhouse, magical meeting place, birdwatcher's hide
- 2 marks for any attempt to rationalise or justify answers, e.g. evidence of footsteps in trampled grass, bird toys

### Question 5: What *would* Kay's Gran and Dad say? (3 marks)

- 1 mark for realising they would tell her to keep away and come home
- 1 mark for articulating the sense of danger
- 1 mark for any extension to this, e.g. realising they would warn her against wandering off, especially without telling them first

### Question 6: About how old is Kay, and how do you know? (3 marks)

- 1 mark for 7–11
- Up to 2 marks for evidence: young enough to be playing on the swing and visiting Gran, but old enough to climb fences and to be adventurous and independent

> Add up the marks out of 10 for Questions 4–6.
> This is the score for **Section B: Responding to Reading**.

### Question 7: What is a *sudden whim* (line 5)? (3 marks)

- 1 mark for getting the gist (e.g. 'rushes off' 'just like that')
- A further mark for a sense of it being an impulse (e.g. 'just because she feels like it', 'does it without thinking')
- A further mark if the answer is well defined (e.g. 'acts on impulse' 'on the spur of the moment')

### Question 8: What does *skittered* mean (line 8)? (2 marks)

- 1 mark for the sense of noise and movement
- A further mark for a word that pinpoints the quality of the noise and movement, e.g. scrabbling

### Question 9: What is a *clearing* (line 11)? (2 marks)

- 1 mark for open space
- A further mark for cleared of trees

### Question 10: What does the last sentence mean? (3 marks)

- 1 mark for explaining that she understood her own desires
- 1 mark for explaining that she trusted her own instincts
- 1 mark for explaining that she was committed now to try the door

> Add up the marks out of 10 for Questions 7–10.
> This is the score for **Section C: Reading Strategies**.

# TEST 2

# Tarantula

Tarantulas are big hairy spiders that live in warm places such as jungles and deserts. They have large heads and jaws, and bodies that can spin silk like other spiders. They are hairy all over. They have 8 legs with 2 tiny claws at the end of each one. Each leg has 7 small moving parts. Tarantulas can grow to be the size of a big dinner plate.

## Hunting

Tarantulas do not spin webs to catch their food like other spiders. They run to catch their food. They hunt at night. They have fangs and use them to grab small animals such as frogs and bugs, and even birds. They crush their prey with their jaws or they can inject venom that makes the flesh melt. They then suck it in. Sometimes they grind their food into a ball and cover it with silk to keep it for later. But no tarantula has ever killed a human being.

## Did you know?

- There are 800 types of tarantula.
- They can be kept as pets.
- They can hiss.
- They have 8 eyes.
- They sleep for most of the day.
- They lay 500–1000 eggs once a year.
- They can live for over 30 years.
- They use their hairs to feel and smell.

## What to do if a tarantula bites you

The bite will swell up and itch, then fade away. Clean the bite with soap and water. Pick out any small hairs, as these cause itching. Use antiseptic.

**HRP Teacher's Resource: Level 2 → 3**

## Questions about tarantulas

1  Label the body parts.

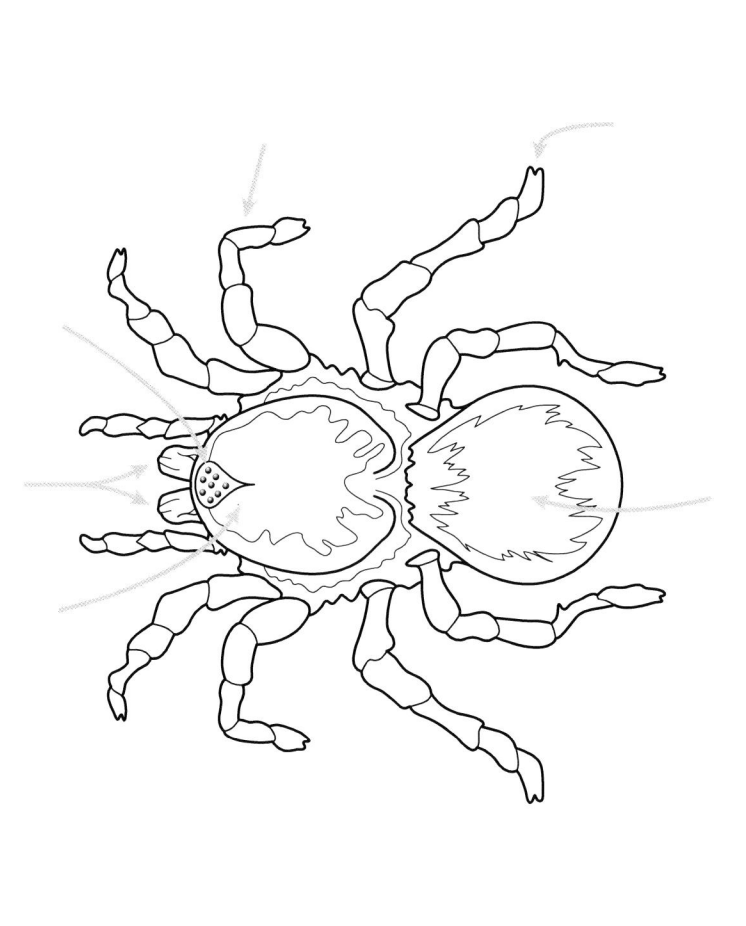

2  What did you find out about the hair of the tarantula?

3  Make notes (no more than 15 words) about the way a tarantula kills its prey.

## Questions about books

4  Where do you find the contents list in a book?

5  What do you use a book index for?

6  Give 3 ways of checking that a book is a good choice for you.

7  Write a review of a book, film or TV programme.

# Test 2: Mark scheme

## Question 1: Label the body parts. (3 marks)

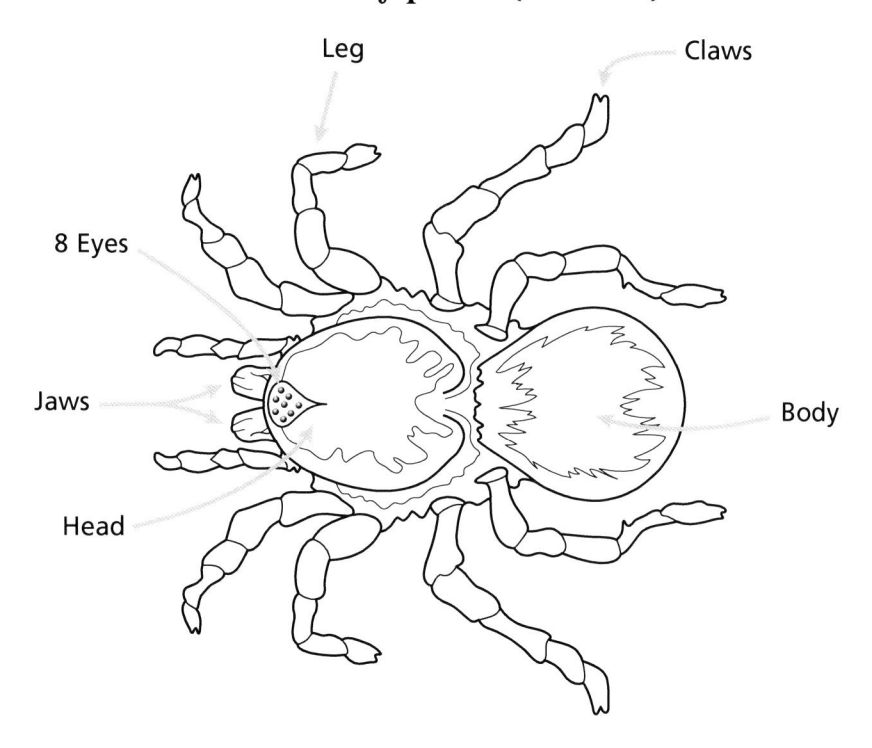

[Diagram of a tarantula with labels: Leg, Claws, 8 Eyes, Jaws, Head, Body]

- Half a mark for each label provided

## Question 2: What did you find out about the hair of the tarantula? (2 marks)

- Give half a mark for each of:
  → they are hairy all over
  → they use hair to feel
  → they use hair to smell
  → the hairs are itchy when they get on the skin

## Question 3: Make notes (no more than 15 words) about the way a tarantula kills its prey. (3 marks)

- 1 mark for the use of a helpful format or diagram such as a flow chart
- 2 marks for getting in the main information: chase – grab – crush or use venom – suck in or save

## Question 4: Where do you find the contents list in a book? (1 mark)

- 1 mark for near the beginning of a book

## Question 5: What do you use a book index for? (1 mark)

- 1 mark for looking up topics to see where they are in the book

> Add up the marks out of 10 for Questions 1–5.
> This is the score for **Section D: Finding What You Need**.

**HRP Teacher's Resource: Level 2 → 3**

### Question 6: Give 3 ways of checking that a book is a good choice for you. (3 marks)

- 1 mark for studying the cover – title, pictures, blurb, etc.
- 1 mark for browsing and sampling paragraphs to get a feel for the language
- A further mark for any other sensible suggestion, e.g. asking other people for a recommendation, consulting a review or asking a librarian

### Question 7: Write a review of a book, film or TV programme. (7 marks)

- 1 mark for each of these features:
  → it gives key facts, e.g. title, author
  → it says what sort of story or text type it is, e.g. horror, true life
  → it indicates the subject matter or plot
  → it comments on the style, language or telling of it
  → it identifies something positive about it
  → it identifies something less pleasing
  → it gives a clear recommendation

Add up the marks out of 10 for Questions 6 and 7.
This is the score for **Section E: Literature**.

# Class Record of Progress

Class _____

| Class names | Test 1 |||| Test 2 ||| Test total | Masterclasses in the Pupil's Book |||||||||||||||| Test 3 ||| Test 4 || Test total | Improvement |
|---|---|---|---|---|---|---|---|---|---|---|---|---|---|---|---|---|---|---|---|---|---|---|---|---|---|---|---|---|
| | A | B | C | D | E | | | A1 | A2 | A3 | B4 | B5 | B6 | C7 | C8 | C9 | D10 | D11 | D12 | E13 | E14 | E15 | A | B | C | D | E | | |

HRP Teacher's Resource: Level 2 → 3

# Pupil Record of Progress

Name _____
Class _____

| Score | Test 1 A | Test 1 B | Test 1 C | Test 2 D | Test 2 E | Test total | Masterclasses in the Pupil's Book A1 | A2 | A3 | B4 | B5 | B6 | C7 | C8 | C9 | D10 | D11 | D12 | E13 | E14 | E15 | Test 3 A | Test 3 B | Test 3 C | Test 4 D | Test 4 E | Test total | Improvement |
|---|---|---|---|---|---|---|---|---|---|---|---|---|---|---|---|---|---|---|---|---|---|---|---|---|---|---|---|---|
| 10 | | | | | | | | | | | | | | | | | | | | | | | | | | | | |
| 9 | | | | | | | | | | | | | | | | | | | | | | | | | | | | |
| 8 | | | | | | | | | | | | | | | | | | | | | | | | | | | | |
| 7 | | | | | | | | | | | | | | | | | | | | | | | | | | | | |
| 6 | | | | | | | | | | | | | | | | | | | | | | | | | | | | |
| 5 | | | | | | | | | | | | | | | | | | | | | | | | | | | | |
| 4 | | | | | | | | | | | | | | | | | | | | | | | | | | | | |
| 3 | | | | | | | | | | | | | | | | | | | | | | | | | | | | |
| 2 | | | | | | | | | | | | | | | | | | | | | | | | | | | | |
| 1 | | | | | | | | | | | | | | | | | | | | | | | | | | | | |
| 0 | | | | | | | | | | | | | | | | | | | | | | | | | | | | |

Colour in your score.

© Hodder Murray 2006. Hodder Reading Project: Level 2–3

# STEP 2
# Set personal reading targets for Level 2–3 readers

The results of the initial test can be used to set personal targets for pupils. Select their weakest sections for attention.

For convenience, photocopiable cards have been provided on page 22. You can give these to pupils for their reference. Laminated on card, they look and feel like credit cards. There are three cards per section.

Each group of personal targets is addressed in the Pupil's Book. You will find them in the aims at the start of each masterclass. Remember that each masterclass concludes with a further mini-assessment. This will tell you and your pupils how well they are doing between the main before-and-after tests.

# Target cards

| A1 Reading targets: Seeing what you read | A2 Reading targets: What next? | A3 Reading targets: Feeling it |
|---|---|---|
| • To 'see' what you read<br>• To spot clues the writer gives me<br>• To imagine what happens | • To use clues to say how a story will end<br>• To work out what will happen next<br>• To guess how the characters will behave | • To put yourself in someone else's shoes<br>• To think how people feel<br>• To understand what makes them tick |
| **B4 Reading targets: Using your experience** | **B5 Reading targets: Thinking aloud** | **B6 Reading targets: Reading like a detective** |
| • To use your past experience when you read<br>• To remember other books when you read<br>• To make guesses based on experience | • To think about what you read<br>• To ask yourself questions about what you read<br>• To be an active reader | • To find clues and put them together<br>• To see things you are not told in so many words<br>• To build up a picture of what is happening |
| **C7 Reading targets: Sounding out words** | **C8 Reading targets: Working out words** | **C9 Reading targets: Reading longer sentences** |
| • To sound out tricky words<br>• To tackle tricky letter clusters<br>• To tackle tricky vowel sounds | • To break long words into easy bits<br>• To work out a word from the context<br>• To work out what parts of a word mean | • To look at the shape of longer sentences<br>• To see the main meaning of long sentences<br>• To chunk up long sentences for easier reading |
| **D10 Reading targets: Finding information** | **D11 Reading targets: Seeing what's there** | **D12 Reading targets: Making notes** |
| • To find the kind of book you need<br>• To check if a book can give you what you need<br>• To find the part of the book you need | • To see at a glance what a page is about<br>• To see how pages are laid out<br>• To find the main points on a page | • To decide what to keep as notes<br>• To make your notes short<br>• To choose a good way to show your notes |
| **E13 Reading targets: Choosing a novel** | **E14 Reading targets: Writing a book review** | **E15 Reading targets: Answering test questions** |
| • To choose books that are right for you<br>• To read and use book covers<br>• To sample the story when you find a book | • To say what you think about books<br>• To explain your opinions<br>• To write good book reviews | • To think what test questions want from you<br>• To find answers to test questions<br>• To explain your answers to test questions |

© Hodder Murray 2006. Hodder Reading Project: Level 2–3

# STEP 3
# Use the Pupil's Book to teach and to track progress

Having established the strengths and weaknesses of pupils' individual reading, you will have a good idea of the spread of needs across your class.

→ If you have **a class composed of readers mainly at this level**, it might make sense to use the Pupil's Book as a unit of work on Reading Strategies, working through the masterclasses over a number of weeks. You can lead the lessons, and use the text as your guide and resource. The activities are sufficiently varied to allow for this, and there is time to include starters at the beginning of each lesson. Having completed the book, you could organise the class into groups with similar personal targets and allocate the appropriate reading books. Rotate around the groups, and time your contribution to coincide with the particular activities that address their priorities.

→ If your **class contains a wider range of reading abilities**, you have two choices. First, you could teach the masterclasses which feature the most common priorities, then split the class into reading ability groups. Some could move on to the reading books whilst others continue to look at further masterclasses relevant to their needs. For example, only a handful of pupils may need help with vocabulary and word attack skills. They could be grouped together to follow masterclasses C7: Sounding out words you don't know, and C8: Working out words you don't know. Ideally, they would be led through these masterclasses by you or an assistant, but if you do not have that level of staffing, the Pupil's Book is written to allow pupils to work independently.

→ Whichever way you organise the class, you know that both the Pupil's Book and the reading books are designed to be flexible and to allow pupils to work alone or in groups.

→ Each masterclass in the book ends with an **assessment task**. This task draws on the skills introduced in the masterclass. The mark scheme is provided on the same page for two good reasons: so that pupils will scan ahead to see what they need to do to succeed, and also to encourage peer-marking. Peer-marking is useful because it reinforces a sense of what constitutes success, and because it gives pupils access to other pupils' attempts at the same task. Record the marks in the **Class Record of Progress**, and note in particular how pupils perform in relation to their personal targets.

→ If you are following the whole Pupil's Book with the whole class, the **Class Record of Progress** allows you to monitor progress from the initial tests, through the assessment tasks in each masterclass and in the concluding tests. But pupils also can follow their progress on their own **Pupil Record of Progress**. A photocopiable master can be found on page 20. Ask pupils to colour in their scores so it looks like a thermometer.

23

HRP Teacher's Resource: Level 2 → 3

# Teaching plans for the Pupil's Book

The five sections of the Pupil's Book constitute approximately 6 hours of teaching each, though the pace of delivery is flexible. Although the Pupil's Book is aimed at pupils with low reading ages, it does cover a number of objectives from the current year. These are listed below.

The whole scheme can also be used with Years 5 and 6 and pending the review of the NLS Framework for Teaching Objectives the relevant primary objectives will be available at www.hodderreadingproject.co.uk from Spring 2006 onwards.

## A The Reading Experience

### Aims of this unit of work

- To enhance readers' visualisation of the text
- To stimulate prediction
- To promote empathetic responses to the text

### Objectives addressed (by year)

**Year 7 objectives**

R6 Active reading
R15 Endings
R17 Independent reading
S&L12 Exploratory talk

**Year 8 objectives**

R4 Versatile reading
R5 Trace developments

**Year 9 objectives**

R13 Evaluate own reading

### Delivery

The unit is organised in three masterclasses of around 2 hours each:

Masterclass 1: Seeing what you read
Masterclass 2: What next?
Masterclass 3: Feeling it

Total: 6 hours

**Teaching plans for the Pupil's Book**

## B Responding to Reading

### Aims of this unit of work

- To encourage readers to refer to their own experience to help them make sense of the text
- To prompt readers to interrogate the text
- To stimulate the skills of inference and deduction

### Objectives addressed (by year)

**Year 7 objectives**

| | |
|---|---|
| R6 | Active reading |
| R8 | Infer and deduce |
| R12 | Character, setting and mood |
| S&L1 | Clarify through talk |
| S&L12 | Exploratory talk |

**Year 8 objectives**

| | |
|---|---|
| R4 | Versatile reading |
| R7 | Implied and explicit reading |
| Wr3 | Writing to reflect |
| S&L5 | Questions to clarify or refine |
| S&L10 | Hypothesis and speculation |

**Year 9 objectives**

| | |
|---|---|
| R8 | Readers and texts |
| R13 | Evaluate own reading |

### Delivery

The unit is organised in three masterclasses of around 2 hours each:

Masterclass 4: Using your experience
Masterclass 5: Thinking aloud
Masterclass 6: Reading like a detective

Total: 6 hours

## C Reading Strategies

### Aims of this unit of work

- To develop phonics for use with longer and more complex words
- To develop strategies for working out the meaning of unfamiliar words
- To develop strategies for making sense of longer and more complex sentences

### Objectives addressed (by year)

**Year 7 objectives**

- **Wd1** Vowel choices
- **Wd10** Analogy
- **Wd16** Unfamiliar words
- **Sn3** Boundary punctuation

**Year 8 objectives**

- **Wd1a** Vowel choices
- **Wd1c** Word endings
- **Wd1d** Prefixes and suffixes
- **Wd6d** Sounds and syllables
- **Wd6f** Word formation
- **Wd6g** Analogy
- **Wd7a** Word families
- **Wd7b** Unfamiliar words

**Year 9 objectives**

- **Wd4b** Apply knowledge

### Delivery

The unit is organised in three masterclasses of around 2 hours each:

Masterclass 7: Sounding out words you don't know
Masterclass 8: Working out words you don't know
Masterclass 9: Reading longer sentences

Total: 6 hours

**Teaching plans for the Pupil's Book**

## D Finding What You Need

### Aims of this unit of work

- To improve research and selection skills
- To develop scanning strategies to appraise content
- To improve the choice and use of notes

### Objectives addressed (by year)

**Year 7 objectives**

| | |
|---|---|
| R1 | Locate information |
| R2 | Extract information |
| R4 | Note-making |
| R7 | Identify main ideas |
| Wr2 | Planning formats |

**Year 8 objectives**

| | |
|---|---|
| R3 | Note-making formats |
| R10 | Development of key ideas |

**Year 9 objectives**

| | |
|---|---|
| R1 | Information retrieval |
| R3 | Note-making at speed |
| Wr2 | Exploratory writing |

### Delivery

The unit is organised in three masterclasses of around 2 hours each:

Masterclass 10: Finding information
Masterclass 11: Seeing what's there
Masterclass 12: Making notes

Total: 6 hours

# E Literature

## Aims of this unit of work

- To help pupils choose novels which are well matched to their interests and abilities in reading
- To introduce pupils to the conventions of writing a formal book review
- To prepare pupils for tackling the reading questions in the test

## Objectives addressed (by year)

**Year 7 objectives**

R17   Independent reading
Wr19  Reflective writing

**Year 8 objectives**

R12   Independent reading
Wr18  Critical review

**Year 9 objectives**

R5    Evaluate own critical writing
Wr3   Formal essay
Wr17  Cite textual evidence

## Delivery

The unit is organised in three masterclasses of around 2 hours each:

Masterclass 13: Choosing a novel
Masterclass 14: Writing a book review
Masterclass 15: Answering test questions

Total: 6 hours

# STEP 4
# Use the reading books to apply and consolidate learning

The reading books are selected for older readers whose reading levels lie between Levels 2 and 3. Half of the books are suitable for pupils still within Level 2 and half are suitable for pupils who are edging into Level 3.

The reading books have been selected because they exercise the skills and strategies taught in the Pupil's Book. This means that you can use them to apply and consolidate those skills in a genuine reading context.

Each book has a **Reading instructions sheet** to help pupils pace their reading by stopping at certain staging points to work on activities which address the skills and strategies taught in the Pupil's Book. Ideally, the reading of books will be organised in groups so that pupils can read aloud and work on activities together.

The tables on pages 30 and 31 show which books offer opportunities to practise which skills.

**HRP Teacher's Resource: Level 2 → 3**

## Matching Level 2 texts to skills and strategies

| Skills and strategies | Fiction 1 *The Underground* | Fiction 2 *Shop Till You You Drop* | Information 1 *Ant & Dec* | Information 2 *Martin Luther King* | Play 1 *Place Your Bets* | Play 2 *I Never Done Nothing* |
|---|---|---|---|---|---|---|
| **A1** Seeing what you read | ✓ | | | | | ✓ |
| **A2** What next? | ✓ | ✓ | | | ✓ | ✓ |
| **A3** Feeling it | | ✓ | | | ✓ | |
| **B4** Using your experience | | ✓ | | ✓ | ✓ | ✓ |
| **B5** Thinking aloud | | ✓ | | | ✓ | ✓ |
| **B6** Reading like a detective | ✓ | ✓ | | ✓ | | ✓ |
| **C7** Sounding out words you don't know | ✓ | | | | | ✓ |
| **C8** Working out words you don't know | | | ✓ | ✓ | ✓ | ✓ |
| **C9** Reading longer sentences | ✓ | | | | | ✓ |
| **D10** Finding information | | | ✓ | ✓ | | |
| **D11** Seeing what's there | ✓ | | | | ✓ | ✓ |
| **D12** Making notes | | | ✓ | ✓ | | ✓ |
| **E13** Choosing a novel | ✓ | | | | | |
| **E14** Writing a book review | ✓ | | | | | |
| **E15** Answering test questions | ✓ | ✓ | ✓ | ✓ | ✓ | ✓ |

## Matching texts to skills and strategies

### Matching Level 3 texts to skills and strategies

| Skills and strategies | Fiction 1 *Foul Play* | Anthology 1 *Urban Myths* | Information 1 *The Black Death* | Information 2 *You won't believe this but...* | Anthology 2 *Mini-sagas* | Fiction 2 *The Red Fox* |
|---|---|---|---|---|---|---|
| **A1** Seeing what you read | | ✓ | ✓ | | ✓ | ✓ |
| **A2** What next? | ✓ | ✓ | | | ✓ | ✓ |
| **A3** Feeling it | ✓ | ✓ | ✓ | | ✓ | ✓ |
| **B4** Using your experience | ✓ | ✓ | | ✓ | ✓ | |
| **B5** Thinking aloud | | ✓ | | ✓ | ✓ | |
| **B6** Reading like a detective | | ✓ | | ✓ | ✓ | ✓ |
| **C7** Sounding out words you don't know | | | ✓ | | | ✓ |
| **C8** Working out words you don't know | ✓ | | ✓ | ✓ | | ✓ |
| **C9** Reading longer sentences | | | | | | ✓ |
| **D10** Finding information | | | ✓ | | | ✓ |
| **D11** Seeing what's there | ✓ | | | | | |
| **D12** Making notes | | | ✓ | | | |
| **E13** Choosing a novel | | | ✓ | | | |
| **E14** Writing a book review | ✓ | | ✓ | | | |
| **E15** Answering test questions | ✓ | ✓ | ✓ | ✓ | ✓ | ✓ |

# Introducing the books to groups

First, put pupils into groups of similar ability and need (based on the information gleaned from Tests 1 and 2). If you are focusing on specific skills, you will select appropriate books for them to work through. A group of three to five works best.

Next, distribute the books and the relevant **Reading instructions sheet**, enough for one each. If the book has other supporting worksheets, this is probably the best time to distribute them. This avoids sudden demands for photocopies later on.

Explain that the group should work together by taking turns to read aloud and by stopping off to undertake the activities on the **Reading instructions sheet**. Point out how the sheet works – they read a short section, then stop for discussion. You could ask the group (or a capable member of it) to organise turns in reading, or allocate a teaching assistant to support them. It is helpful if pupils take charge of their own reading as far as possible.

The pupils should now take turns to read aloud in their groups – a section, page or paragraph, depending on their skill.

The main task of any supporting adult is to prompt and support the use of reading strategies such as the use of sounding out, context and other word attack skills. It is not only useful but important to ask pupils how they process hesitations and what they do when they get stuck. It is also important to ask first for sounding out, to avoid guesswork at the expense of accuracy.

If the group has a shared focus such as a common target, then there will be opportunities to discuss and practise it. It is tempting for adults to move on quickly by providing answers. However, it is not always the best solution with these pupils, who have failed to learn by picking things up as they go. Your fluency does not resolve their reading problem. A better course is to stop at a convenient moment and tackle reading hesitations assertively and explicitly. Ask how something works, how problems may be tackled, exemplify a strategy and ask for explanations and demonstrations. Pay close attention to the text, because all the clues are there: the hints that lead to visualisation, the sounds in words, the grammatical logic of a sentence, the progress of the narrative, and so on.

Draw the pupils in to articulate how they work on the toughest tasks in reading. When a pupil gets stuck, you could ask:

- *Can we break it into sounds?*
- *How would you go about cracking this?*
- *Can anyone see clues that would help?*
- *What should David try first?*
- *What else could he try?*

Also respond to successes:

- *I liked the way you used (a strategy) to work that out.*
- *Tell us how you worked out that difficult word, David.*

## Introducing the books to groups

Invite other pupils to help out when a pupil gets stuck, but preferably by prompting them rather than doing it for them. In this way, pupils learn to help themselves.

You may not have someone to help you. Once the groups have the hang of it, and are settled, they can work alone. This will free you to visit them at a useful point. At first you may want to preside over the class until it is on task, but after that it is recommended that you spend substantial time with each group rather than flitting between them. If you have a teaching assistant, it may be appropriate to allow that person to oversee the class, field questions, offer occasional help and manage low-level behaviour issues. This will allow you to concentrate on teaching.

To prepare to work with a group, it would be helpful if you and any assistant could:

1. Read the book (done in very few minutes).

2. Scan the worksheet and decide when you would be best to join the group. If they have a common target, then you will choose the questions that address it.

3. Remember when you allocate the groups to ask them to alert you when they are up to that section.

4. Join the group in the expectation that you will steer but they will do the work. Expect the ratio of talk to be 1:3 (you:them).

# STEP 5
# Reassess pupils at the end of the scheme

You may now wish to retest pupils to compare them against their skills at the start of the scheme. Another two simple tests along the lines of Tests 1 and 2 can be found on pages 35–36 and 39–41. Like these initial tests, they cover all five sections of the scheme and come in two photocopiable papers (Test 3 and Test 4), for which you should allow approximately 30 minutes each in conditions as close as possible to timed silence. The process is identical to that for Tests 1 and 2 outlined on page 10. The mark schemes can be found on pages 37–38 and 42–43.

Afterwards, you can fill in the result for each section into the **Class Record of Progress** (on page 19), and reset targets as necessary.

The next part of this reading scheme addresses pupils moving from Level 3 to Level 4.

# TEST 3

# The Barn

Jack pushed open the door of the old barn and went in. Dan went in after him. It was dark and cold and it smelt, but it was dry.

Both boys peeled off their sopping tops and dropped their heavy bags. It was good to stop and to be out of the rain.

'Where are we, then?' asked Dan.

'No idea,' said Jack. 'We lost the path and then we lost the map. I really don't know.'

'It's a bit creepy in here,' said Jack.

The boys peered into the darkness and very soon their eyes got used to the shade. They made out soft shapes and dark shadows, big heaps of straw and dusty boxes.

In one dark corner they saw a pile of barrels, ropes and chains hanging down, rusty tools with long blades and big hooks in the wall.

The place was covered in cobwebs. The floor was a carpet of thick dust without footprints. It was so still they could hear each other breathe. It felt as if the barn was watching them.

'Look!' cried Dan. 'Look! Something's moving over there!' He pointed into the shadows across the room.

Extract continues on the next page.

In the corner, a dark shape rose up. It swayed and turned. Dan was fixed to the spot, his mouth wide open. His eye was fixed on a rope slung over a beam, and hanging down where the shape had begun to rotate. His mind was racing. 20

'What's that?'

Jack smiled and he did not stop smiling and he did not move. He smiled and smiled until Dan knew that something was very, very wrong. 25

## Questions

1 What had happened to the boys before they came into the barn?

2 Draw the dark corner.

3 What is going on in Dan's mind as he looks at the shape, and what makes you think that?

4 How do you know that the place has been empty for a long time?

5 What makes the place creepy?

6 How does Dan know that something is *very, very wrong* at the end?

7 What does *sopping* mean (line 3)?

8 What does *swayed* mean (line 19)?

9 What does *rotate* mean (line 22)?

10 What does the writer mean by *It felt as if the barn was watching them* (line 16)?

## Test 3: Mark scheme

### Question 1: What had happened to the boys before they came into the barn? (2 marks)

- 1 mark for realising they had got lost, perhaps whilst out walking in the country
- 1 mark for realising they were caught in the rain and needed shelter

### Question 2: Draw the dark corner. (4 marks)

- Half a mark each for:
  - barrels
  - chains
  - ropes
  - a rope slung over a beam
  - rusty tools with long blades
  - big hooks in the walls
  - a swaying shape
  - the effect of dust and cobwebs

### Question 3: What is going on in Dan's mind as he looks at the shape, and what makes you think that? (4 marks)

- 1 mark for recognising the sense of fear
- 1 mark for recognising that he is frozen in shock or terror (*fixed to the spot, his mouth wide open*)
- 2 marks for realising that he is thinking of something sinister or supernatural, such as a ghost

> Add up the marks out of 10 for Questions 1–3.
> This is the score for **Section A: The Reading Experience**.

### Question 4: How do you know that the place has been empty for a long time? (4 marks)

- 1 mark for cobwebs
- 1 mark for carpet of dust
- 1 mark for absence of footprints
- 1 mark for the tools are rusty

### Question 5: What makes the place creepy? (4 marks)

- 1 mark for each stock device from the horror genre, such as:
  - the dust and cobwebs
  - the dark
  - the silence
  - the sinister equipment – ropes, blades, etc.
  - the sinister atmosphere (*It felt as if the barn was watching them*)

### Question 6: How does Dan know that something is *very, very wrong* at the end? (2 marks)

- 2 marks for realising that Jack's fixed smile has gone on for too long to mean amusement

> Add up the marks out of 10 for Questions 4-6.
> This is the score for **Section B: Responding to Reading**.

### Question 7: What does *sopping* mean (line 3)? (2 marks)

- 1 mark for understanding they were wet
- A further mark for getting a sense that they were completely soaked

### Question 8: What does *swayed* mean (line 19)? (2 marks)

- 1 mark for a sense of movement
- A further mark for a sense of it being a slow, sideways, wavering movement

### Question 9: What does *rotate* mean (line 22)? (2 marks)

- 2 marks for turning round and round

### Question 10: What does the writer mean by *It felt as if the barn was watching them* (line 16)? (4 marks)

- Give 1 mark each for:
  - a sense that they were not alone, that someone or something was watching their actions
  - a sense of threat, insecurity or risk
  - an understanding that it might just be in their imaginations
  - a guess at the cause, e.g. supernatural trap

> Add up the marks out of 10 for Questions 7–10.
> This is the score for **Section C: Reading Strategies**.

# TEST 4

## Cobra

The cobra is one of the biggest snakes. It grows up to 5 metres long and has a wide hood around its head. The hood makes it look bigger and scares off other animals. It has black beady eyes, a forked tongue and it hisses and spits.

The cobra is a shy snake and hides away from danger, but if it is afraid, it will hiss and flare its hood. If this does not scare off the attacker, it will spit venom over 2 metres into the attacker's eyes. This is very painful and the victim goes blind for a few hours.

The cobra uses its fangs to bite and kill. The bite of a cobra can kill an elephant in 3 hours, and a person in 15 minutes. The cobra eats small animals such as mice, and even other snakes. It has no 'eating' teeth, so it swallows its victims alive and in one go. The cobra does not need to eat for many days after a meal.

The female cobra lays about 30 eggs in the spring. When they are born, they are already half a metre long and ready to hunt.

Extract continues on the next page.

## ? Did you know?

- The cobra is the snake used by snake charmers.
- Venom is a kind of saliva.
- The venom is injected through the fangs.
- The cobra smells by using its tongue to taste the air.
- Like all snakes, it sheds its skin to allow it to grow.
- The hood has ribs to hold it out.

## What to do if a cobra bites you

Stay calm and try not to move. This will help to stop the venom moving round the body. Clean the bite with water and put antiseptic on it. Tie a band above the bite to slow the blood flow round the body. Wrap a warm cloth around the bite. If it is on an arm or leg, make a splint to stop it moving. Get to a doctor quickly.

## Questions about cobras

1 Label the parts of the body.
2 Make notes (no more than 15 words) about the way a cobra reacts to danger.

3  Fill in the boxes to show what to do if a cobra bites you.

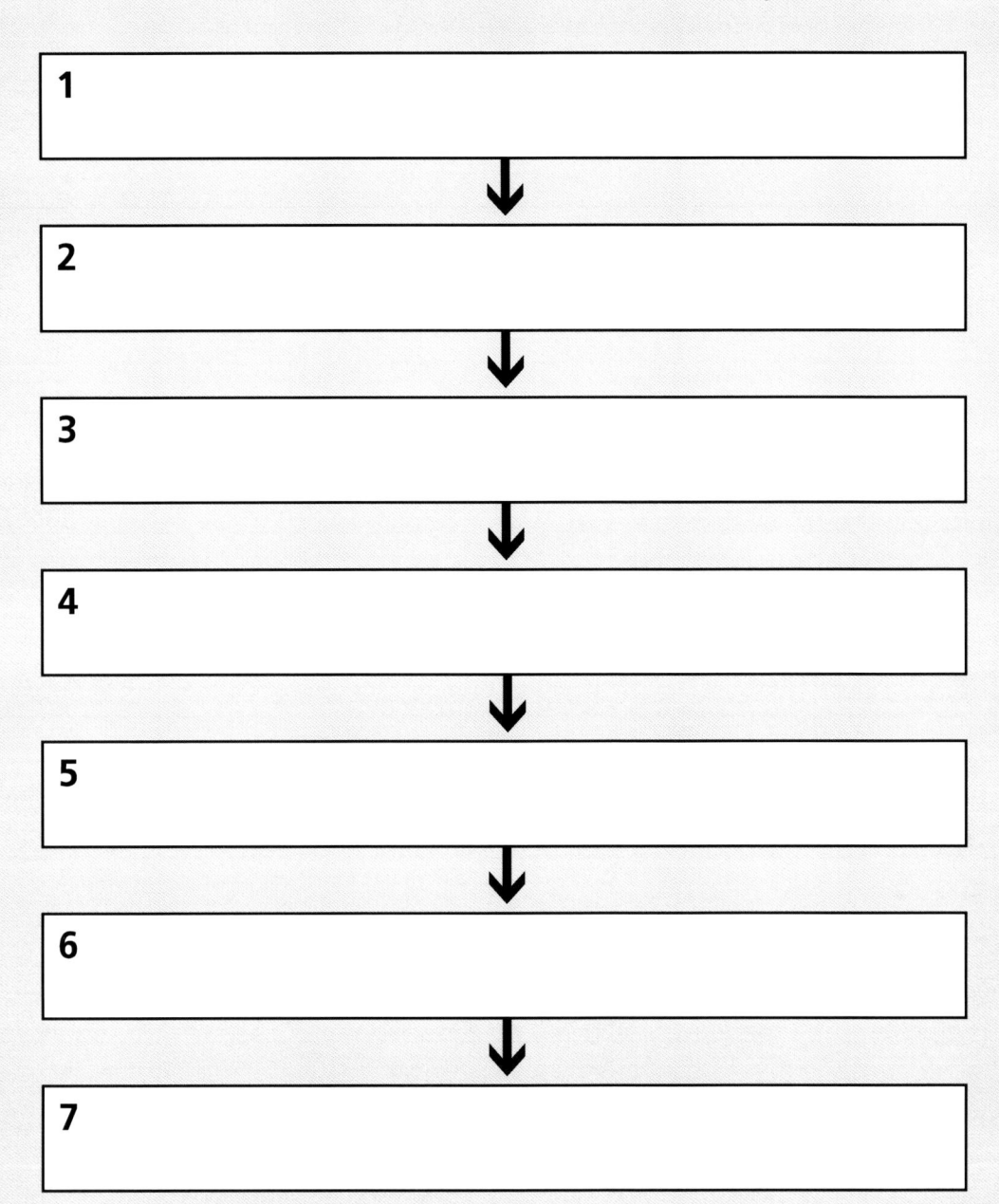

| 1 |
|---|
| ↓ |
| 2 |
| ↓ |
| 3 |
| ↓ |
| 4 |
| ↓ |
| 5 |
| ↓ |
| 6 |
| ↓ |
| 7 |

## Questions about books

4  Where do you find the index in a book?

5  What is listed in the contents page?

6  Give 3 ways of checking that a book is a good choice for you.

7  Write a review of a book, film or TV programme.

## Test 4: Mark scheme

### Question 1: Label the parts of the body. (2 marks)

- Half a mark each for:
  → hood
  → eyes
  → fangs
  → tongue

### Question 2: Make notes (no more than 15 words) about the way a cobra reacts to danger. (2.5 marks)

- Half a mark for each of these in the right order:
  → hides
  → hisses
  → flares its hood
  → spits venom
  → bites

### Question 3: Fill in the boxes to show what to do if a cobra bites you. (3.5 marks)

- Half a mark each for:

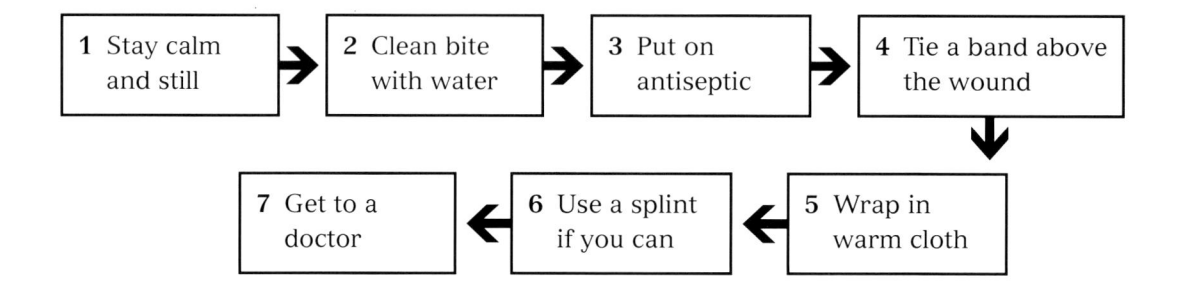

| 1 Stay calm and still | → | 2 Clean bite with water | → | 3 Put on antiseptic | → | 4 Tie a band above the wound |
|---|---|---|---|---|---|---|

| 7 Get to a doctor | ← | 6 Use a splint if you can | ← | 5 Wrap in warm cloth |
|---|---|---|---|---|

### Question 4: Where do you find the index in a book? (1 mark)

- 1 mark for near the back of a book

### Question 5: What is listed in the contents page? (1 mark)

- Half a mark for the chapter or section titles
- Half a mark for the page they start on

> Add up the marks out of 10 for Questions 1–5.
> This is the score for **Section D: Finding What You Need**.

# Test 4: Mark scheme

## Question 6: Give 3 ways of checking that a book is a good choice for you. (3 marks)

- 1 mark for studying the cover – title, pictures, blurb, etc.
- 1 mark for browsing and sampling paragraphs to get a feel for the language
- A further mark for any other sensible suggestion, e.g. asking other people for a recommendation, consulting a review or asking a librarian

## Question 7: Write a review of a book, film or TV programme. (7 marks)

- 1 mark for each of these features:
  - it gives key facts about it, e.g. title, author
  - it says what sort of story or text type it is, e.g. horror, true life
  - it indicates the subject matter or plot
  - it comments on the style, language or telling of it
  - it identifies something positive about it
  - it identifies something less pleasing
  - it gives a clear recommendation

Add up the marks out of 10 for Questions 6 and 7.
This is the score for **Section E: Literature**.

HRP Teacher's Resource: Level 2 → 3

# Information about the reading books, including photocopy masters

## Level 2

### 1 The Underground
### by Brandon Robshaw

### Synopsis

A simple horror story in which a young woman gradually realises she is on an underground journey to Hell. Victim of a terrible mistake, she begs to be allowed home, but officials find a neat way of securing her compliance. The book ends as it starts – a recurrent nightmare.

### This reading book follows up these masterclasses

- A1: Seeing what you read
- A2: What next?
- B6: Reading like a detective
- C7: Sounding out words you don't know
- C9: Reading longer sentences
- D11: Seeing what's there
- E13: Choosing a novel
- E14: Writing a book review
- E15: Answering test questions

### You will need

- Sheet 1.1: Reading instructions (pp.45–48)

### Extension teaching points

- Similar plots in the horror genre
- The idea of recurrence (e.g. *Groundhog Day*, *It's a Wonderful Life*)
- Symbolism, e.g. of the underground
- Drama opportunity to act out the events of the next day

Level 2: The Underground

## The Underground
### Reading instructions

Sheet 1.1

## Before reading

- Work out from the cover what kind of story this will be.

- Think of a reason why the writer called it *The Underground* rather than *The Tube*.

## Read Chapter 1

- Find 5 ways the writer makes it feel spooky.

- What does line 4 on page 1 mean? Why does the writer choose those words?

- *Cold* and *grey* (in line 6 on page 1) are words that hint at sadness and death. Can you find 3 more words like them?

## Read Chapter 2

- What do you think the last line on page 4 means?

- What makes you worry about it?

- What do you think will happen next?

- Look back at the lines which ran on over one line, into the next line. How do you read long sentences? How do you look ahead to see what's coming?

- *Carriage* in line 1 on page 3 is an odd spelling. Why is there an *i* in it? Can you think of other words that have the same ending?

## Read Chapter 3

- This chapter ends with a scare and you don't know what caused it. Why do writers of horror stories do this?

## Read Chapter 4

- Draw Boris's face using the words on page 7.

- *He looked like a dead man* is a simile, because it compares one thing with another. Find another simile in the chapter.

# HRP Teacher's Resource: Level 2 → 3

- Besides his looks, what other clues tell you that Boris is dead?
- Find 5 more 'horror' words.
- What will happen next?
- Look at the box below before reading Chapter 5.

> **Read this...**
>
> ### Before reading Chapter 5
>
> Try this trick to get an overview of Chapter 5.
>
> Read ahead, but only read the first line of each paragraph. This is skimming. It will give you a quick idea of the story.
>
> Is there any bit that doesn't make sense? If so, try reading the bit just before it, to get the idea.

## Read Chapter 5

- Did skimming give you a fair idea of what it was about?
- Who are *the Authorities*, do you think?

## Read Chapter 6

- Why are the signs in red?
- Why is it getting colder and colder?
- Find 4 more details that give you a bad feeling.
- What details about the man tell you that he isn't going to help her?

Level 2: The Underground

## Read Chapters 7 and 8

- Think of 3 different endings.

- The word *brightened* on page 25 is based on what word? What does it mean here?

- Find 2 examples of a long sentence. When you read them, how did you look ahead for the meaning?

## Read Chapter 9

- Find the words repeated from Chapter 1.

- Explain what has happened.

- The word *though* on page 28 makes the 'o' sound with 4 letters (*-ough*). Can you think of other words that end in the same way?

## After reading

- Horror stories have similar ingredients such as:
  - cold, dark, grey places
  - bad weather
  - monsters
  - people back from the dead
  - the supernatural
  - forces of evil
  - being trapped or cornered
  - history repeating itself

- Can you think of examples from films and stories?

- Can you see examples in this book?

- Can you think of other ingredients?

- Write a book review (see Help box on page 48).

## Help

**Book reviews**
**Reviews tell you:**

The title, author and any key facts
↓
What sort of book it is
↓
What it is about
↓
How it is told (the style)
↓
What is good about it
↓
What might put you off
↓
If you recommend it

See Masterclass E14: *Writing a book review* in the Pupil's Book for help.

- Go and look at the horror shelf in the library. Spot:
  - ▶ popular topics
  - ▶ popular writers
  - ▶ what often appears on covers
  - ▶ similarities in the titles
- Work out which sort you like best and pick one to read and review.

# Level 2: Shop Till You Drop

## 2 Shop Till You Drop by John Goodwin

### Synopsis

Lucy is persuaded by her friend to try on clothes she can't afford to buy, and eggs her on with promises of new-found popularity if she spruces herself up. Lucy begins to feel dissatisfied with her image, and uses her mother's credit card to buy the clothes she craves. But the shopping spree comes to an end when Lucy's mother receives a bill and confronts Lucy with what she has done. The clothes go back and the book finishes with Lucy at home, missing the disco she had been preparing for, and in repentant mood.

### This reading book follows up these masterclasses

- A2: What next?
- A3: Feeling it
- B4: Using your experience
- B5: Thinking aloud
- B6: Reading like a detective
- E15: Answering test questions

### You will need

- Sheet 2.1: Reading instructions (pp.50–51)
- Sheet 2.2: The people (p.52)
- Sheet 2.3: Jenna (p.53)
- Sheet 2.4: Lucy (p.54)
- Sheet 2.5: Lucy's mum (p.55)

### Extension teaching points

- There are opportunities to go beyond the text here to research:
  → money crimes such as fraud, counterfeit and stealing
  → peer pressure
  → wanting things badly
- There are opportunities to explore alternative scenarios, and some of these are suggested in the instructions

HRP Teacher's Resource: Level 2 → 3

## Shop Till You Drop
### Reading instructions

Sheet 2.1

**You will need:**

Sheet 2.2: The people

Sheet 2.3: Jenna

Sheet 2.4: Lucy

Sheet 2.5: Lucy's mum

## Before reading

- Find out what a credit card is and how it works.

- List crimes that are to do with money, e.g. theft.

## Read up to the end of Chapter 2

- On Sheet 2.2 write the names of the 3 people in the story so far.

- Find 3 figures of speech.

- Jenna is pushy. Find 3 examples to prove it.

- What do you really know about Jez?

## Read up to the end of Chapter 4

- What does Lucy mean when she says of her clothes that *they were me*? Can you think of things that feel like 'you'?

- The writer does not tell the reader much about Jenna but you can work it out. Write words that describe Jenna around her picture on Sheet 2.3. Show your proof in the next box.

- Lucy commits a crime. But what makes her do it? Fill in the bubbles on Sheet 2.4 to show what she is thinking.

- Find 3 places where the writer tells you how things feel to the touch. Why does he do it?

**Level 2: Shop Till You Drop**

## Read up to the end of Chapter 6

- Where do you begin to see that Lucy has lost control?

- How does the writer give you a feel for Lucy's needy feelings?

- Add more names to Sheet 2.2.

- What do these clues tell you:

  ▸ *I'd stuff it all in my wardrobe, until it was overflowing* (page 16)

  ▸ *Their chins practically bounced off their work tables* (page 16)

  ▸ *It was in a bright red colour* (page 18)

  ▸ *I banged the poker on the ash until it was dust* (page 20)

- What is the most likely ending to this story, and why?

## Read up to the end of the book

- Where is the moment when you know the game is up? Point to the clue.

- Think about Lucy's mum and how she must have felt when she saw the bill. Fill in the bubbles on Sheet 2.5.

- Act out some other ways that the talk between Lucy and her mum could have gone. Compare what happens in the story. Did Lucy's mum handle it well, or not?

## After reading

- Choose parts for Jenna, Jez, Tariq and a teacher.
  At school the next day, everyone is talking about Lucy. Act out what they say. Tariq can start by saying, 'Have you heard about Lucy Snedden …?' and the teacher can finish it by telling them to get off to the next lesson.

- Discuss what Jenna, Lucy and her mum could have done to help Lucy and stop her making her big mistake?

- Write another part of the play when Lucy goes back to school.

**HRP Teacher's Resource: Level 2 → 3**

## Sheet 2.2

### The people

# Sheet 2.3: Jenna

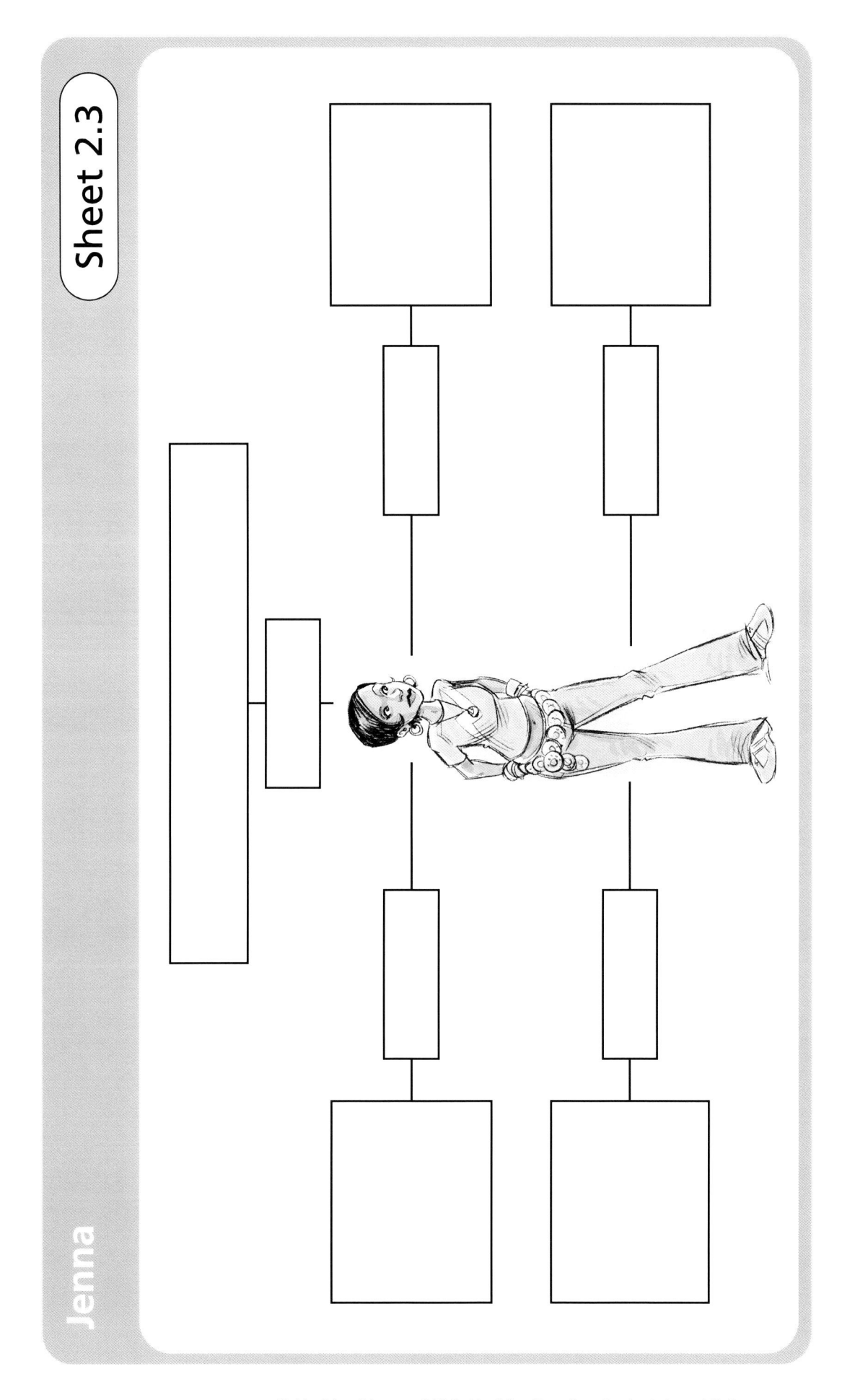

Level 2: Shop Till You Drop

# Lucy

Sheet 2.4

**Level 2: Shop Till You Drop**

# Lucy's mum

Sheet 2.5

**HRP Teacher's Resource: Level 2 → 3**

## 3 Ant & Dec by Andy Croft

### Synopsis

The book traces the career of Ant and Dec, including interesting personal details about their backgrounds.

### This reading book follows up these masterclasses

- C8: Working out words you don't know
- D10: Finding information
- D12: Making notes
- E15: Answering test questions

### You will need

- Sheet 3.1: Reading instructions (pp.57–58)
- Sheet 3.2: Map (p.59)
- Sheet 3.3: Family trees (p.60)
- Sheet 3.4: Timeline (p.61)

### Extension teaching points

- There are opportunities to go beyond the text here to:
  → reflect on what makes things funny
  → study a show
  → compare other show business duos
- There are also opportunities to experiment with presentations to a camera

Level 2: Ant & Dec

## Ant & Dec
### Reading instructions

Sheet 3.1

**You will need:**

Sheet 3.2: Map

Sheet 3.3: Family trees

Sheet 3.4: Timeline

## Before reading

- Discuss what you know about Ant and Dec. Work out:
  - how old you think they are
  - where they come from
  - what they are like

## Read Chapters 1–3

- Find Newcastle in an atlas and mark it on the map (Sheet 3.2).
- Fill in the names on the family trees (Sheet 3.3).
- Fill in dates on the timeline (Sheet 3.4).
- Name 5 things that Ant and Dec have in common.
- What is their appeal? In other words, what is it about them that makes people like them?
- Use your word skills to guess what Psychandrics are (page 7).

## Read Chapters 4–6

- Fill in more dates on the timelines.
- Ant and Dec have had 4 different roles during their careers. What are they? Give an example of each one.

© Hodder Murray 2006. Hodder Reading Project: Level 2–3

## Read Chapters 7–9

- Fill in more dates on the timeline.

- Which of the shows do you remember?

- Some of the titles of the shows are jokes. They play on words. Can you explain the titles?

- The writer tells us that Ant and Dec are like twins. But can you say how they are different?

## After reading

- Watch a show with Ant and Dec in it and try to describe their style. Notice how they work together to make jokes.

- Name some other TV comics who work as a pair, such as Morecambe and Wise. Describe their way of working together. How do they compare with Ant and Dec?

- A story is usually organised in time order so that the story moves forward in 'real' time. Factual books can be organised in many different ways, such as by time, topic or alphabet. How is this book organised?

**Level 2: Ant & Dec**

**Map**  Sheet 3.2

# Sheet 3.3

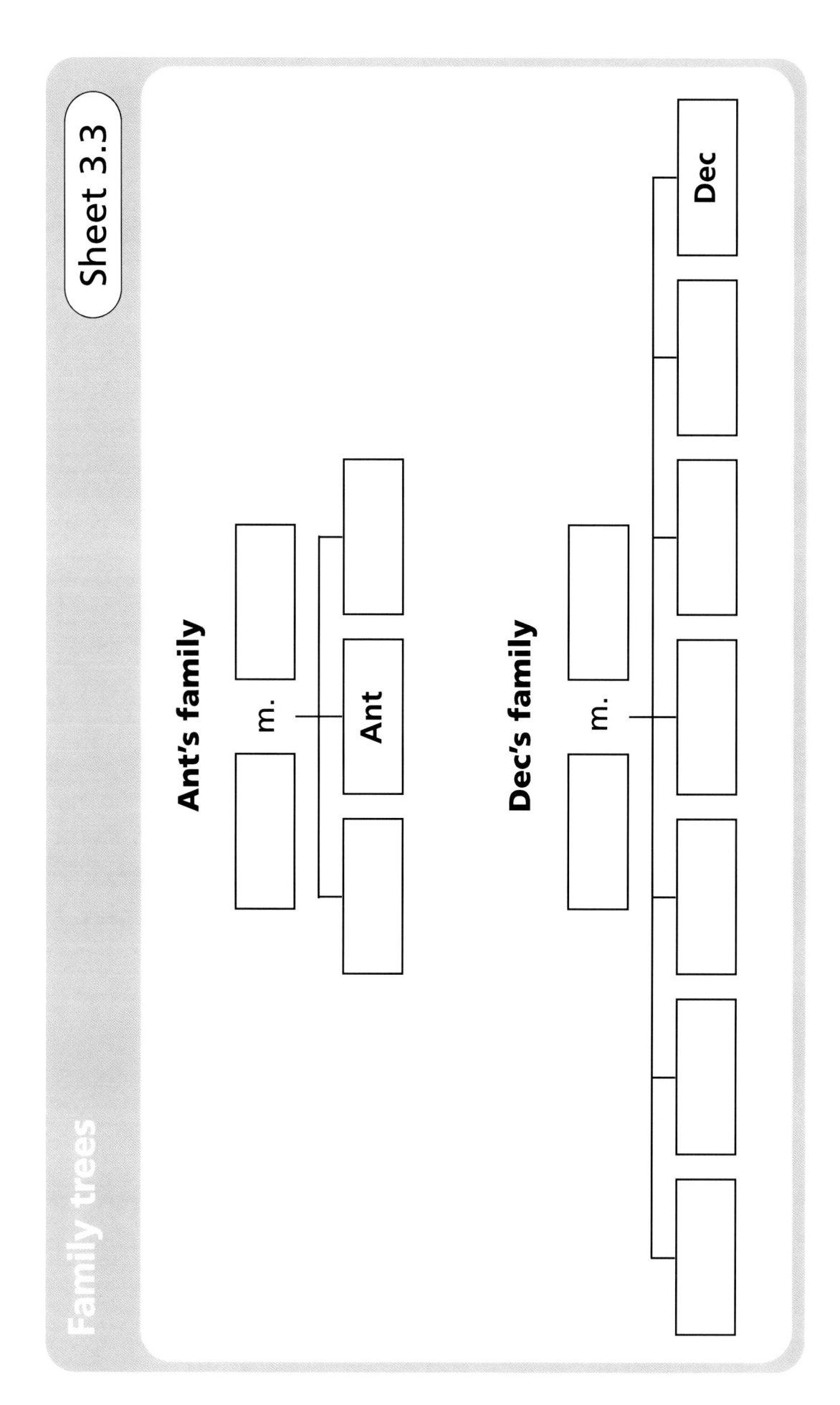

## Family trees

**Ant's family**

m. — Ant

**Dec's family**

m. — ... Dec

**Level 2: Ant & Dec**

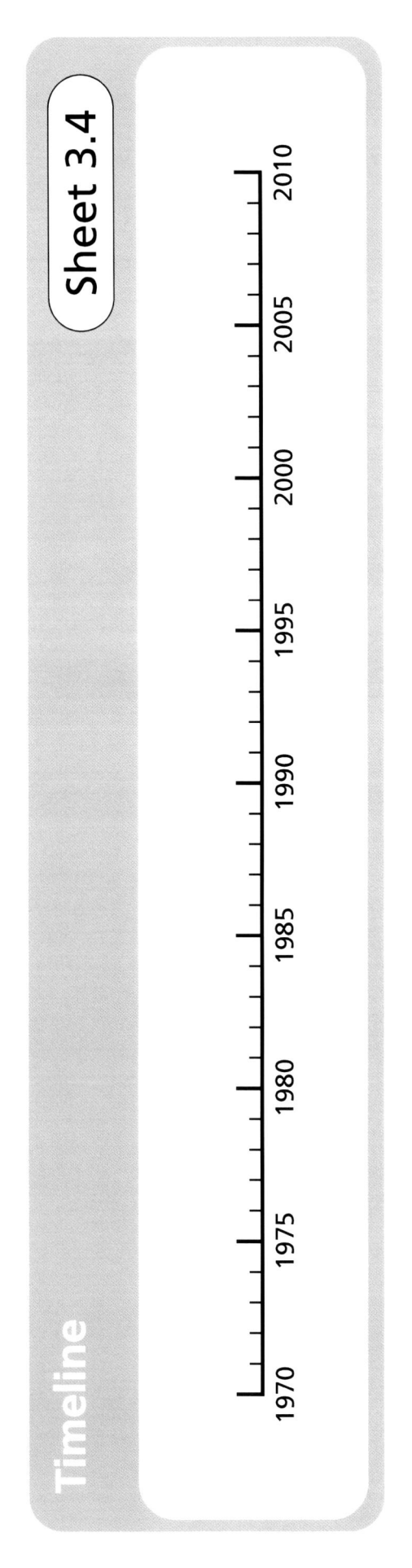

Sheet 3.4

Timeline

1970
1975
1980
1985
1990
1995
2000
2005
2010

© Hodder Murray 2006. Hodder Reading Project: Level 2–3

HRP Teacher's Resource: Level 2 → 3

# 4 Martin Luther King by Julia Holt

## Synopsis

This book traces the life of Martin Luther King and highlights his main achievements, as well as catching personal glimpses of his private life.

## This reading book follows up these masterclasses

- B4: Using your experience
- B6: Reading like a detective
- C8: Working out words you don't know
- D10: Finding information
- D11: Seeing what's there
- D12: Making notes
- E15: Answering test questions

## You will need

- Sheet 4.1: Reading instructions (pp.63–64)
- Sheet 4.2: Map of the United States of America (p.65)
- Sheet 4.3: Timeline (p.66)
- Sheet 4.4: Wall poster (p.67)
- Atlas containing states and cities in the United States of America

## Extension teaching points

- There are opportunities to go beyond the text here to research:
  → the history of slavery
  → the life and work of Gandhi
  → the life and work of John F. Kennedy
  → the subsequent history of black emancipation
  → film footage of King's 'I have a dream' speech
- There are also opportunities to explore in drama:
  → Rosa Parks and the bus strike

Level 2: Martin Luther King

## Martin Luther King
### Reading instructions

Sheet 4.1

**You will need:**

Sheet 4.2: Map of the United States of America

Sheet 4.3: Timeline

Sheet 4.4: Wall poster

Atlas containing states and cities in the United States of America

## Before reading

- Discuss what you already know about Martin Luther King.

- Discuss what you already know about the history of black people in the United States of America.

## Read pages 1 and 2 and look at the picture on page 3

- Find 2 things the picture tells you that the words do not.

## Read up to page 9

- Work out what the following words mean by looking at their parts and the way they are used. Check in the dictionary afterwards.

    ▶ *Civil War* (p.4)

    ▶ *Segregate* (p.4)

    ▶ *Divinity* (p.7)

- Find out where Alabama is and mark it on the map of the United States of America on Sheet 4.2. Use an atlas. Look in the index for Alabama.

- Discuss what you know about Gandhi. Do you know any other people who have fought against segregation?

© Hodder Murray 2006. Hodder Reading Project: Level 2–3

## Read up to page 15

- Work out the meaning of the words:
  - *boycott* (p.11)
  - *hard labour* (p.14)
  - *racists* (p.14)
- Discuss why you think the bus companies gave in.
- What were the reasons behind the hate?
- Find Birmingham and mark it on the map of the United States of America.

## Read up to page 18

- Find Washington and Dallas and mark them on the map of the United States of America.
- Discuss what you already know about John F. Kennedy.
- Discuss what Martin Luther King meant by:
  - the sons of slaves and the sons of slave owners (p.17)
  - the table of brotherhood (p.17)

## Read up to the end

- Find Memphis and mark it on the map of the United States of America.
- The mule cart was a symbol of his humble beginnings. The table of brotherhood was a symbol of peace between the races. A symbol stands for an important idea. Can you find other symbols in the book?

## After reading

- Mark the important dates on the timeline on Sheet 4.3.
- Look back at the photographs and discuss what more they tell you about Martin Luther King.
- Write 25 to 30 words on the Martin Luther King wall poster on Sheet 4.4. Tell people what he did to make us proud of him.

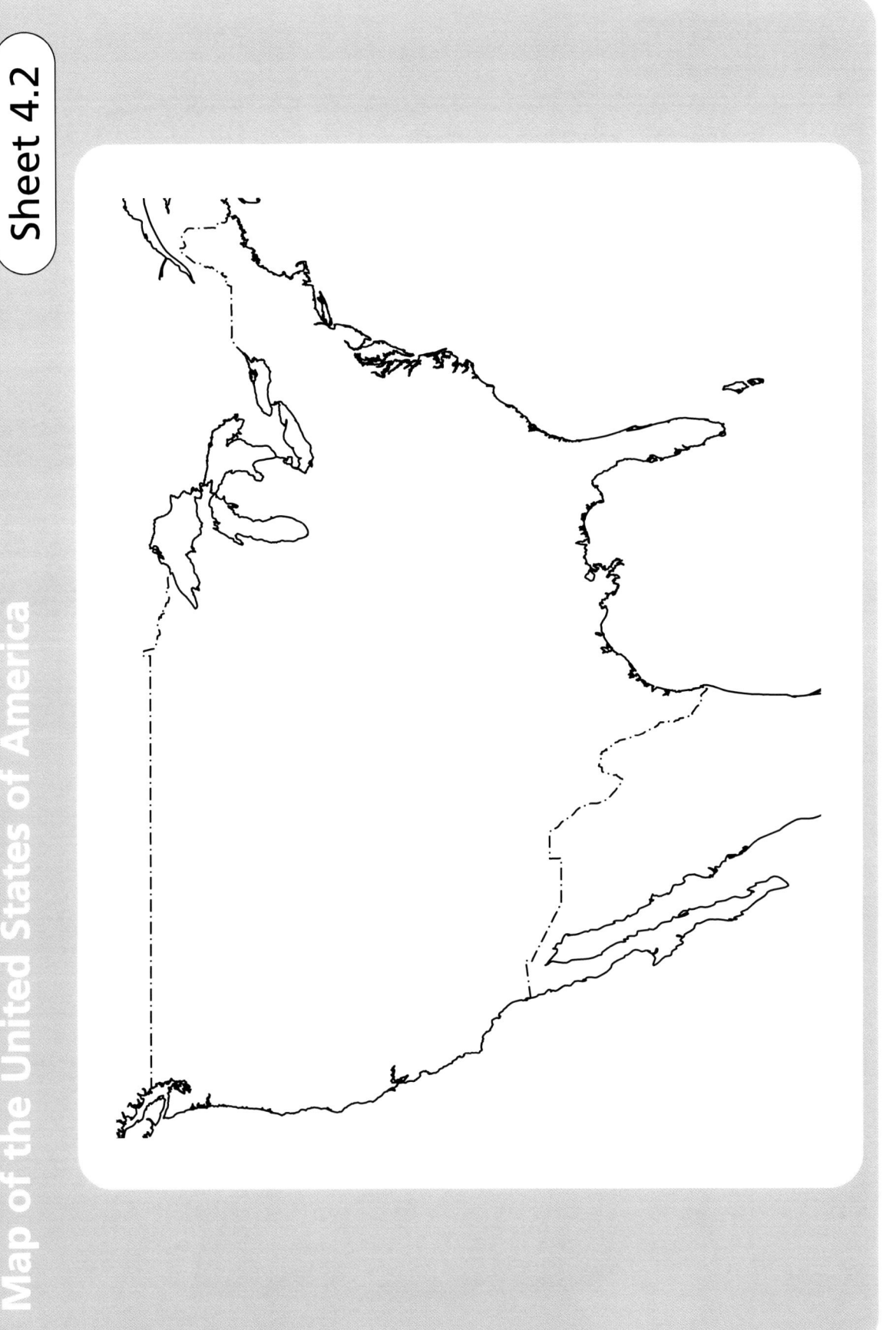

**Level 2: Martin Luther King**

Sheet 4.2

Map of the United States of America

## Sheet 4.3 — Timeline

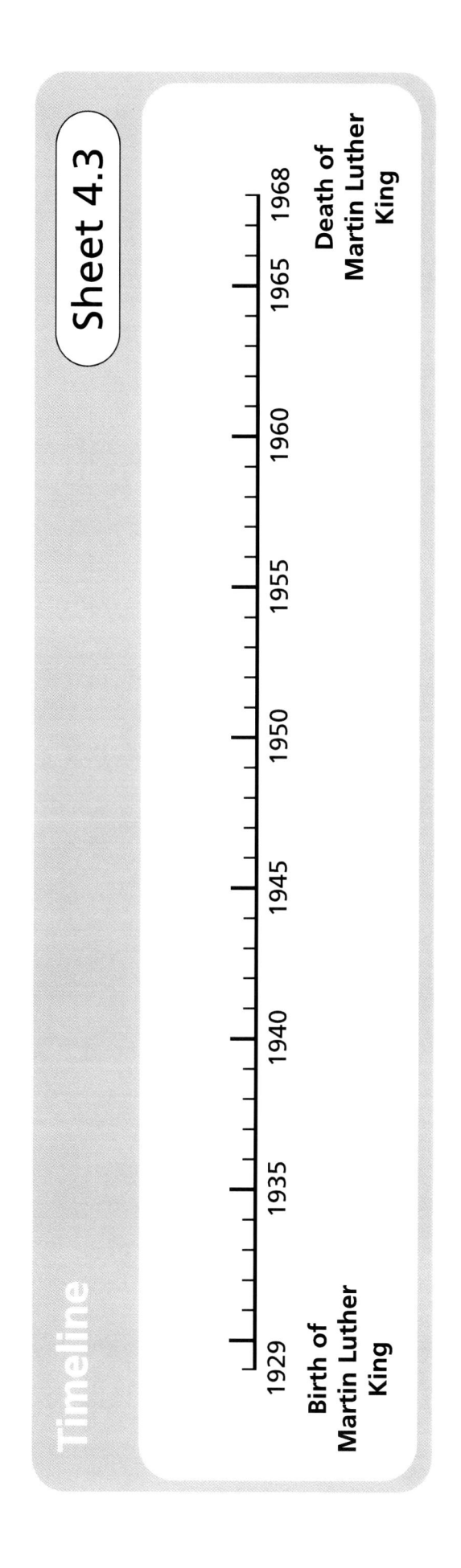

- 1929: Birth of Martin Luther King
- 1935
- 1940
- 1945
- 1950
- 1955
- 1960
- 1965
- 1968: Death of Martin Luther King

Level 2: Martin Luther King

**Wall poster**     Sheet 4.4

# MARTIN LUTHER KING
# 1929–1968

_____
_____
_____
_____
_____

# 5 Place Your Bets by John Goodwin

## Synopsis

**Act 1:** Sisters Emma and Carla think there has been a break-in at their home. A TV and a CD player are missing. But Emma is not sure this is the real explanation: she has another idea about where they have gone.

**Act 2:** Mum gets home and Emma confronts her about the missing items. Despite her initial attempt to deny knowledge, Mum then admits that she has sold them to fund her gambling.

**Act 3:** Carla is surprised to find her CD player back in its place, but it has suffered damage. She wrings the truth from Emma, who has used her own savings to buy back the CD player. They agree to confront their mother.

**Act 4:** The girls confront their mother with an ultimatum: 'Stop gambling or we'll leave.'

**Act 5:** Mum arrives home with a new TV, claiming that she has saved up to buy it and has given up gambling for good.

**Act 6:** Mum repays Emma, presents money to Carla and proposes a summer holiday. But Emma is not taken in. She realises the money has come from a gambling win. Emma begins to pack.

## This reading book follows up these masterclasses

- A2: What next?
- A3: Feeling it
- B4: Using your experience
- B5: Thinking aloud
- C8: Working out words you don't know
- E15: Answering test questions

## You will need

- Sheet 5.1: Reading instructions (pp.69–70)
- Sheet 5.2: Mum (p.71)
- Sheet 5.3: Emma (p.72)
- Sheet 5.4: The end (p.73)

## Extension teaching points

- There are opportunities for discussion, role play and writing playscripts based on the themes of:
  → addictive behaviour – gambling, spending, bingeing, bullying
  → resolving problem behaviour within the family

Level 2: Place Your Bets

## Place Your Bets
### Reading instructions

Sheet 5.1

**You will need:**
Sheet 5.2: Mum

Sheet 5.3: Emma

Sheet 5.4: The end

## Before reading

- List different kinds of gambling.
- Why do some people love to gamble?
- Are some kinds of gambling worse than others? Why?
- Take a part each: Emma, Carla or Mum. Another person can read the words in *italics*.

## Read Acts 1 and 2

- How does Mum try to avoid the hard questions Emma asks her?
- Go back to Act 1 and see how Emma does the same thing to Carla.
- Why do you think gamblers tend to deny they have a problem?
- Why doesn't Emma tell Carla what she really thinks?

## Read Acts 3 and 4

- Explain the words *addict* (page 10) and *addiction*.
- What other things can you be addicted to?
- What leads to addiction?
- Look back at all the things you have picked up about Mum. Write what you know about her in the square boxes on Sheet 5.2.

© Hodder Murray 2006. Hodder Reading Project: Level 2–3

- In the thought bubble on Sheet 5.2, write what Mum is thinking at the end of Act 4.
- In the bubbles on Sheet 5.3, write some of the things Emma is thinking.

## Read Acts 5 and 6

- When exactly does Emma realise that her mum is lying?
- The words *roll over* are used in 2 different ways on pages 23 and 25. Explain the difference.
- Write on Sheet 5.4 what each of them is thinking at the end of the play.
- What might happen next?
- Why is *this* the end of the play?

## After reading

- Act out what happens when Emma and Carla arrive at their dad's.
- Act out a discussion between Mum, Emma and Carla that takes place a few days later.
- What happens at the end of most stories? What do you like to see at the end?
- Why do writers sometimes want to write endings that are not neat and happy?

**Level 2: Place Your Bets**

**Mum**  Sheet 5.2

**HRP Teacher's Resource: Level 2 → 3**

## Emma

Sheet 5.3

# Sheet 5.4

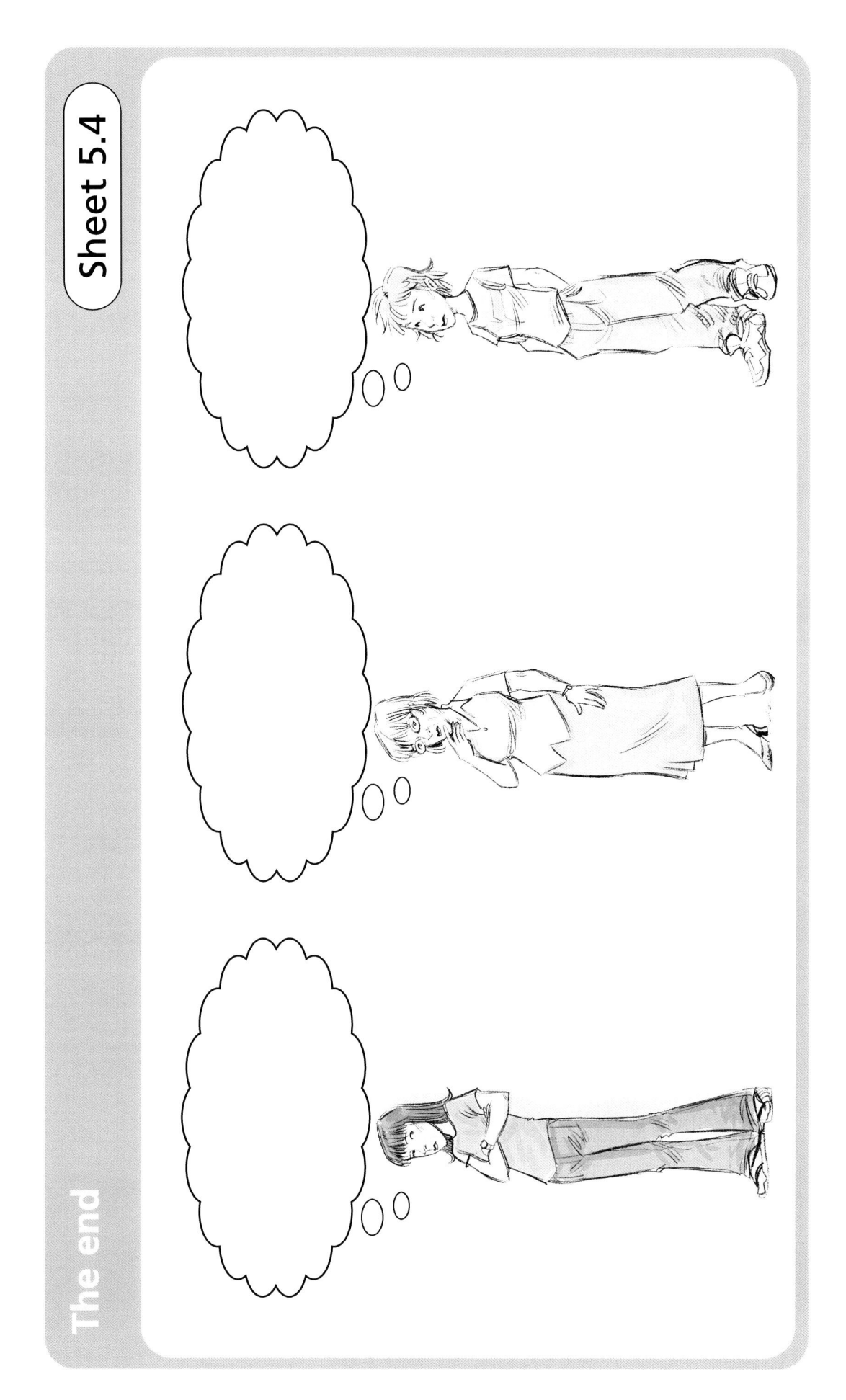

## Level 2: Place Your Bets

**The end**

## 6 I Never Done Nothing
### by Peter Leigh

### Synopsis

A play with two parts – Gary and Raj.

**Act 1:** School friends Raj and Gary are discussing an incident in a club on the previous evening. The humour lies in their bragging and self-deception. Raj has picked a fight with Jon-Paul, which resulted in breakages. He has been thrown out of the club and now can't go there.

**Act 2:** Raj hears from Gary that Jon-Paul – a martial arts enthusiast – is now threatening to beat him up, and an after-school fight has been arranged. Nervously, Raj says he has a detention and goes home quickly.

**Act 3:** Caught at the school gates, Raj is back in school and the time of the fight is approaching. Raj gives Gary some home truths. He has discovered from Jon-Paul that Gary has been stirring things up, trying to get Jon-Paul to take things out on him (Raj). Together, Raj and Jon-Paul decided to teach Gary a lesson by threatening a fight. Gary has been found out, and Raj has changed his allegiances. Gary escapes as quickly as he can.

### This reading book follows up these masterclasses

- A1: Seeing what you read
- A2: What next?
- B4: Using your experience
- B5: Thinking aloud
- B6: Reading like a detective
- C7: Sounding out words you don't know
- C8: Working out words you don't know
- C9: Reading longer sentences
- D11: Seeing what's there
- D12: Making notes
- E15: Answering test questions

### You will need

- Sheet 6.1: Reading instructions (pp.75–76)
- Sheet 6.2: Flow chart (p.77)
- Sheet 6.3: Raj and Gary (p.78)
- Sheet 6.4: Raj's thoughts (p.79)
- Sheet 6.5: Reading aloud (p.80)

### Extension teaching points

- Playwriting based on bragging and its exposure
- Other examples of lies that find you out
- The idea of just deserts

**Level 2: I Never Done Nothing**

## I Never Done Nothing
### Reading instructions

Sheet 6.1

**You will need:**

Sheet 6.2: Flow chart

Sheet 6.3: Raj and Gary

Sheet 6.4: Raj's thoughts

Sheet 6.5: Reading aloud

## Before you read

- Look at the cover. Does it tell you anything about the kind of book this is? Where do you find clues?

- Now look at page iii ('About the Play'), near the front of the book. What more do you know?

## Read Act 1

- Fill in the flow chart on Sheet 6.2. Show the order of events at the club last night.

- Where are the big laughs in this act?
    - ▶ In each case, what or who are you laughing at?
    - ▶ How can an actor make sure the joke gets a laugh?
    - ▶ How does the writer try to make sure it gets a laugh?

- Think of 5 words each to describe Raj and Gary. Then write them on Sheet 6.3.

## Read Act 2

- Raj says, *You don't have to worry about me. I can look after myself* (page 18). Do you believe him, and why?

- What is Raj really thinking? Fill in the bubbles on Sheet 6.4.

- What do you make of Gary? Fill in more words on Sheet 6.3.

© Hodder Murray 2006. Hodder Reading Project: Level 2–3         **75**

- Think of other ways that Raj could have reacted to Gary's news. Then act them out.

- How do you think the play will go from here?

## Read Act 3

- Most stories have the same sort of ending: the hero wins, finds love, defeats evil, gets a reward. What is good about *this* ending?

- What is the moral or message of the story?

- Fill in more words about Raj and Gary on Sheet 6.3.

## After reading

- Try learning your lines and acting out the best bit of the play.

- Note down some tips you used for learning your lines.

- Discuss Sheet 6.5 and fill in your answers.

- Write a new scene, in which Raj and Jon-Paul meet Gary in the bike sheds the next day.

Level 2: I Never Done Nothing

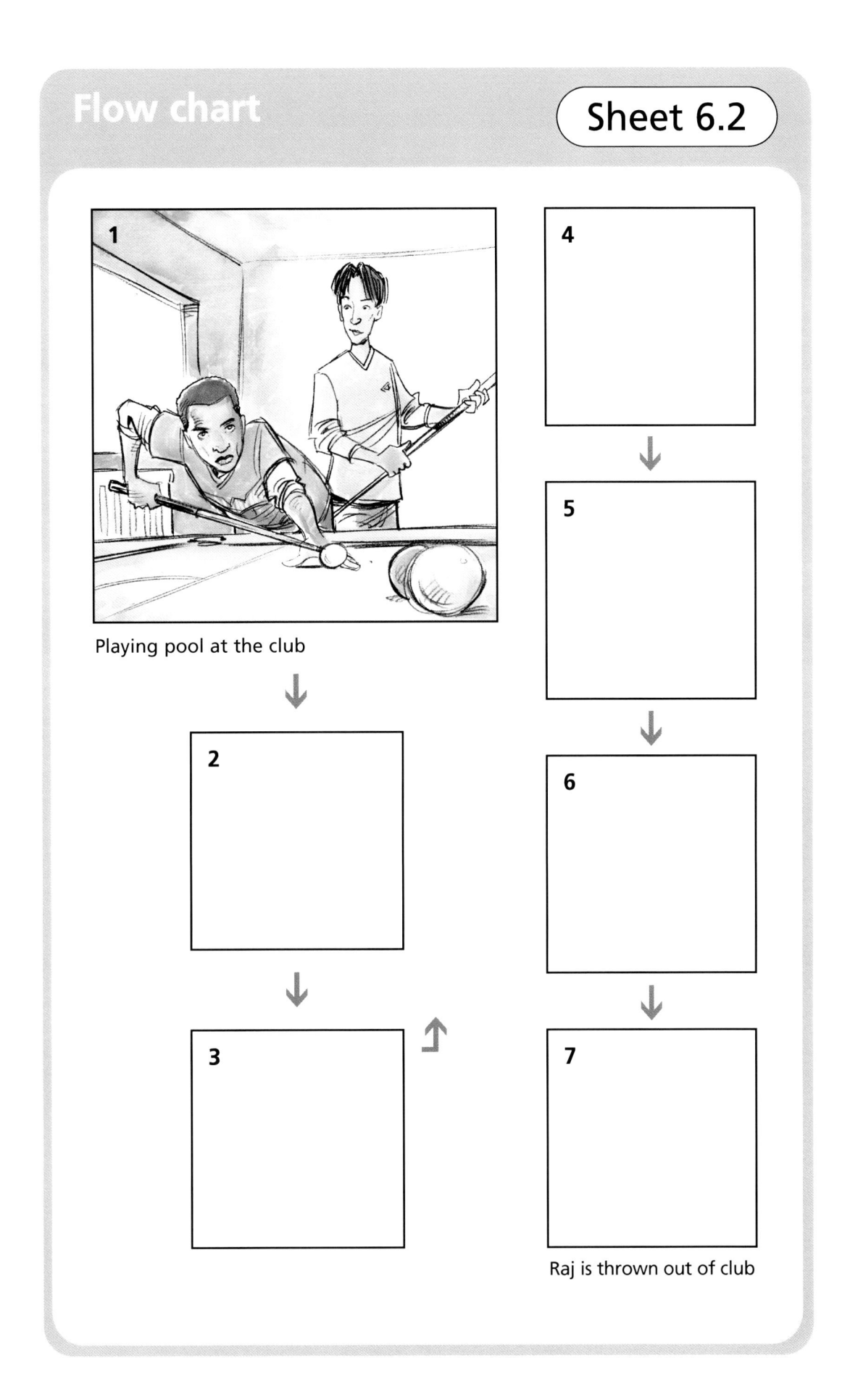

## Flow chart

Sheet 6.2

**1**

Playing pool at the club

**2**

**3**

**4**

**5**

**6**

**7**

Raj is thrown out of club

© Hodder Murray 2006. Hodder Reading Project: Level 2–3

**HRP Teacher's Resource: Level 2 → 3**

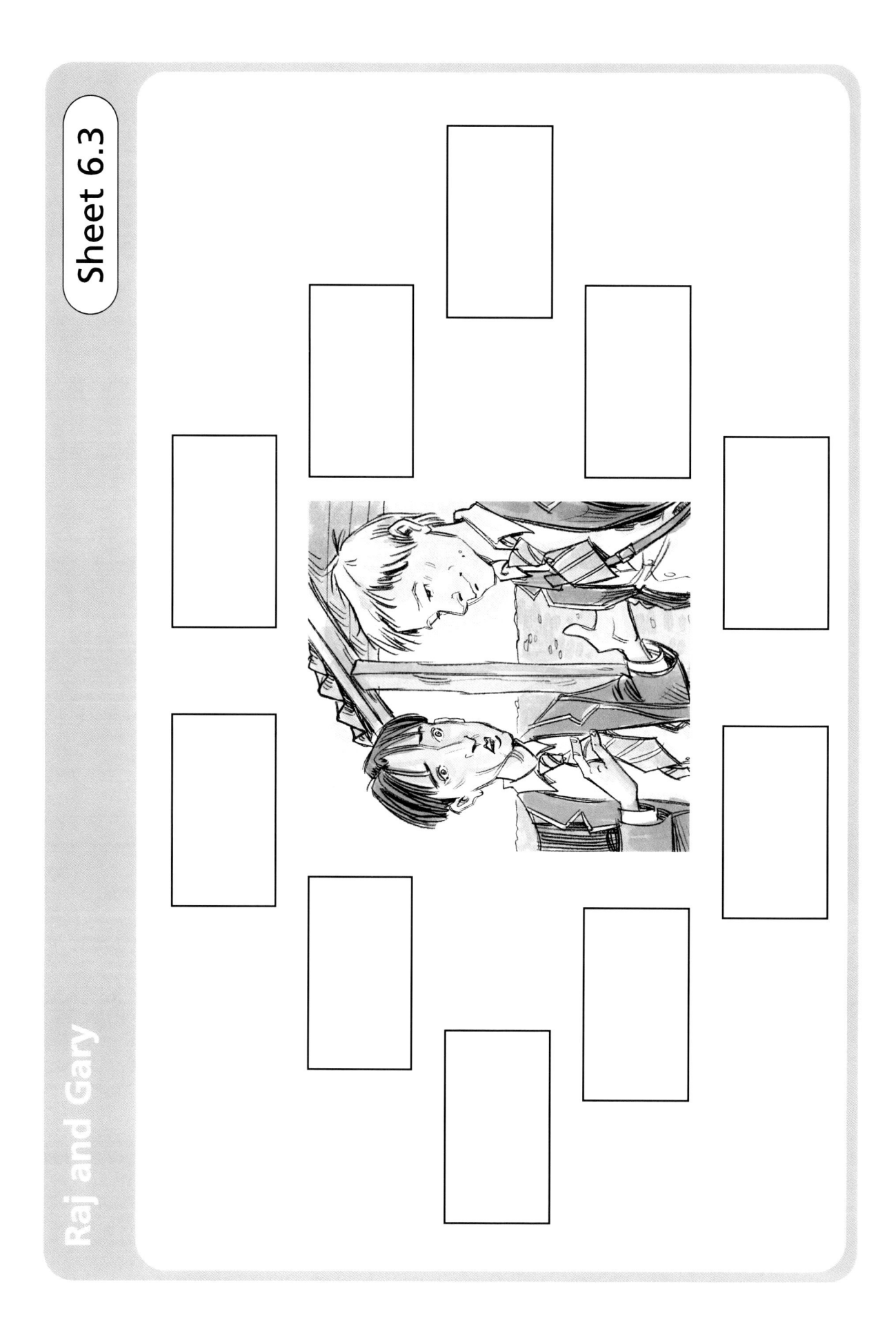

Sheet 6.3

Raj and Gary

Level 2: I Never Done Nothing

**Raj's thoughts**

Sheet 6.4

© Hodder Murray 2006. Hodder Reading Project: Level 2–3

**Reading aloud**

Sheet 6.5

## How did you go about reading aloud your lines?

What happened when you came across a word you didn't know?
Give 3 ways of going about it.

1 _____

2 _____

3 _____

How did you get ready to speak your line at the right time and in the right way?

1 _____

2 _____

3 _____

How did you get ready for a long line? How did you get the sense of it?

1 _____

2 _____

3 _____

What other tips do you have for people reading aloud?

1 _____

2 _____

3 _____

# Information about the reading books, including photocopy masters

## Level 3

### 7 Foul Play by John Goodwin

### Synopsis

**Chapter 1:** Jamie is a keen footballer who is bullied by Chocka and Dezzy.

**Chapter 2:** Chocka and Dezzy refuse to pass the ball to Jamie and cut him out of the game. Jamie misses a free kick when he is distracted by their jeers.

**Chapter 3:** Chocka corners Jamie and uses threats to force him to undertake a robbery.

**Chapter 4:** Reluctantly, Jamie enters a lock-up to steal kit for the bullies. Suddenly the police arrive and Jamie escapes just in time.

**Chapter 5:** Jamie's kit bag is stolen. The PE teacher discovers that Chocka has hidden the bag. It is found, but the shirt in it has been slashed. Chocka is told to provide a new shirt or else!

**Chapter 6:** Jamie is invited to join the school team. Winston, the goalkeeper, comes round to practise with Jamie.

**Chapter 7:** The match. Jamie finally finds his form with the support of Winston. He begins to put the bullies behind him.

### This reading book follows up these masterclasses

- A2: What next?
- A3: Feeling it
- B4: Using your experience
- C8: Working out words you don't know
- D11: Seeing what's there
- E14: Writing a book review
- E15: Answering test questions

### You will need

- Sheet 7.1: Reading instructions (pp.82–84)
- Sheet 7.2: Jamie's character (p.85)

HRP Teacher's Resource: Level 2 → 3

## Foul Play
### Reading instructions

**Sheet 7.1**

**You will need:**
Sheet 7.2: Jamie's character

## Before reading

- Work out from the cover what kind of story this will be.
- The title has a double meaning. Explain.

## Read Chapter 1

- Give another word for:
  - *mocking* (page 2)
  - *thug* (page 2)
  - *sprint* (page 3)
- The word 'I' is not used on page 1. How do you know that you are reading someone's thoughts?

## Read Chapter 2

- What do you find out about Jamie's character? Write words to describe him around the picture on Sheet 7.2.
- Explain why Jamie misses the shot.

## Read Chapter 3

- Name 3 ways that Chocka and Dezzy bully Jamie.
- What is a *lock-up* (page 13)?
- Add 2 more good points about Jamie's character to the picture.
- What do you think will happen next?

**Level 3: Foul Play**

## Read Chapter 4

- Put yourself in Jamie's shoes. Why does he agree to do the robbery?

- What happens on page 17? How do you know?

> **Read this...**
>
> **Before reading Chapter 5**
>
> Try this trick to get an overview of Chapter 5.
>
> Read only the first line of each paragraph.
> This will give you the gist of the story.
>
> Is there any bit that doesn't make sense?
> Read just before and after it to get the idea.

## Read Chapter 5

- *Then it began* (page 18). What is *it* and why is *it* happening?

- What stops bullies?

- There are still 2 chapters to go. What needs to happen to get a happy ending?

- Did reading ahead give you a good sense of the chapter?

## Read Chapter 6

- On page 27, Jamie thinks of it as a war between him and Chocka. Find 6 words or phrases that tell you this.

- Name 2 ways in which the writer is setting up a happy ending.

© Hodder Murray 2006. Hodder Reading Project: Level 2–3

**HRP Teacher's Resource: Level 2 → 3**

## Read Chapter 7

- What does the third line on page 34 tell you about Jamie's state of mind?

- What do the words *I don't know what happened next* on page 35 tell you about Jamie's state of mind?

- What signs are there that Jamie will be able to *handle* Chocka in future (page 36)?

## After reading

- Write a book review.

### Help

**Book reviews**
**Reviews tell you:**

The title, author and any key facts
↓
What sort of book it is
↓
What it is about
↓
How it is told (the style)
↓
What is good about it
↓
What might put you off
↓
If you recommend it

See Masterclass E14: *Writing a book review* in the Pupil's Book for help.

Level 3: Foul Play

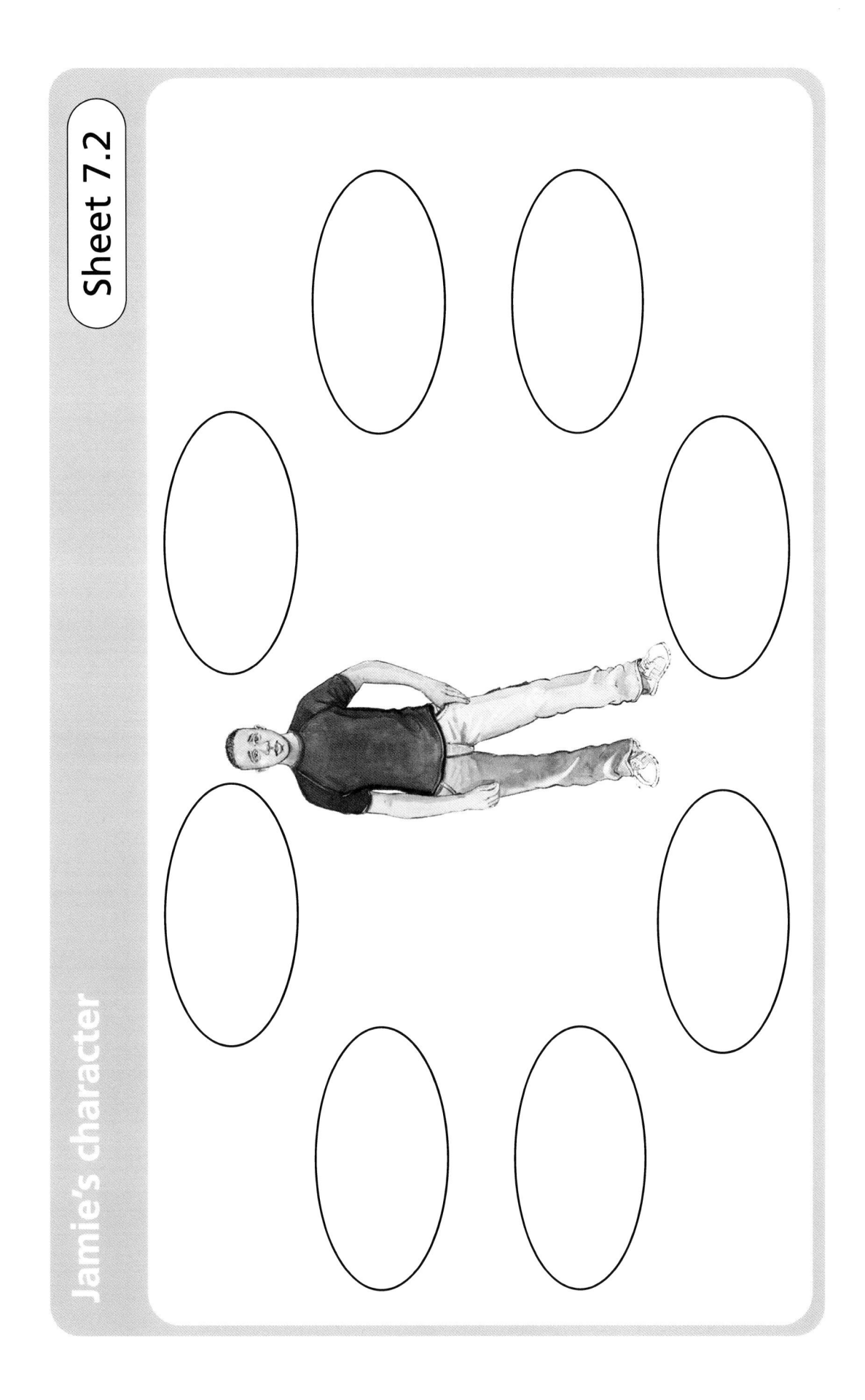

Sheet 7.2

Jamie's character

**HRP Teacher's Resource: Level 2 → 3**

# 8 Urban Myths by Brandon Robshaw and Rochelle Scholar

## Synopsis

The book contains an anthology of modern myths: short, bizarre and intriguing stories which are passed by word of mouth and taken for true, though many of them have been in circulation for centuries. Modern myths strike a chord in the imagination and sometimes touch on common psychological and social anxieties.

## This reading book follows up these masterclasses

- A1: Seeing what you read
- A2: What next?
- A3: Feeling it
- B4: Using your experience
- B5: Thinking aloud
- B6: Reading like a detective
- E15: Answering test questions

## You will need

- Sheet 8.1: Reading instructions (pp.87–89)

## Extension teaching points

- Other stories which meet a social need, e.g. cautionary tales, celebrity gossip, fairy tales, family anecdotes
- Word-of-mouth phenomena – rumours, gossip, 'Chinese whispers', secrets, etc.

Level 3: Urban Myths

## Urban Myths
Reading instructions

Sheet 8.1

## Read Chapter 1

- What is a myth?

- What does *urban* mean?

- Have you been told any spooky stories lately?

## Read Chapter 2: Buried Alive

- Explain why the ending is so chilling.

- Can you think of other stories in which dreams are important?

- How can you tell it is an old story, and not one that was made up recently?

## Read Chapter 3: The Exploding Toilet

- Do you know any other urban myths about toilets?

- What is it about toilets that makes them good for stories like this?

## Read Chapter 4: Bang Bang

- What other stories does this remind you of?

- Why is the setting important?

- Say what you see exactly at the end. You are not told much, but it is a very strong image.

- What strong images are there in the first 2 stories?

## Read Chapter 5: The Rabbit

- What is it in the story that makes you squirm?
- Is anyone to blame?
- What should the man have done?
- Like the other stories, this one ends at the moment when they realise what has happened. What would happen next?
- What would happen next in the other stories so far?
- Why do all urban myths end at the punchline and not say what happens after?

## Read Chapter 6: The Hitch-Hiker

- This is another story about a car in the night in the middle of nowhere. Why do you think this idea is used so often?
- Urban myths often end with an image that says it all. Readers are left to work out the horrible truth for themselves. What is the image in this story? And what is the horrible truth?
- Can you find the same sort of image and horrible truth in 'Bang Bang' and 'Buried Alive'?

## Read Chapter 7: The Kangaroo

- What is the moral of the story?
- What is the moral of 'The Rabbit'?

## Read Chapter 8: Prawns

- Why does the woman smile at the end?
- Why do most readers feel sympathy for the woman rather than her victims?

**Level 3: Urban Myths**

# Read Chapter 9: Spider in the Hair

- This is the oldest story in the book. Why do you think it has been so popular?

- Is there a villain in this story?

# After reading

- Tell each other any other urban myths you know.

- Urban myths are all about our fears. What common fears do they cover?

- Urban fears are often about strong feelings. Find 2 stories about feeling very *embarrassed*. Can you find other feelings?

**HRP Teacher's Resource: Level 2 → 3**

## 9 The Black Death by Sarah Blackmore

### Synopsis

The book contains an accessible factual account of the Black Death, the plague which swept Europe in the 14th century. Full of intriguing and accurate information, the book uses the plague to highlight different aspects of the period including medicine, religious belief and the famous nursery rhyme about the plague, 'Ring O' Roses'.

### This reading book follows up these masterclasses

- A1: Seeing what you read
- A3: Feeling it
- C7: Sounding out words you don't know
- C8: Working out words you don't know
- D10: Finding information
- D12: Making notes
- E13: Choosing a novel
- E14: Writing a book review
- E15: Answering test questions

### You will need

- Sheet 9.1: Reading instructions (pp.91–92)
- Sheet 9.2: Symptoms flow chart (p.93)
- Sheet 9.3: Outline man (p.94)

### Extension teaching points

- Other periods or events in history – such as the Great Fire of London which ended the plague – or the isolated outbreak of plague in Eyam
- The genesis of other nursery rhymes

Level 3: The Black Death

## The Black Death
### Reading instructions

**Sheet 9.1**

**You will need:**
Sheet 9.2: Symptoms flow chart
Sheet 9.3: Outline man

## Before you read

- Look at the cover. What does it tell you about the kind of book this is? Where do you find clues?

- Now flick the pages and look at the contents page near the front. What more do you know?

- What do you already know about the Black Death?

## Read Chapter 1

- What is a *plague*? Where can you find out?

- *Europe* is a hard word to spell. How can you remember the order of the letters?

- Most towns have plague pits. Do you know of one in your area?

## Read Chapter 2

- Name 3 ways that people tried to avoid catching the plague.

- *Temperature* is another word that is hard to spell. What is difficult about it, and how can you learn it?

## Read Chapter 3

- Fill in the flow chart on Sheet 9.2 to show the order in which the symptoms appear.

- Draw and label the symptoms on the outline man on Sheet 9.3.

## Read Chapters 4 and 5

- Imagine you were alive during the plague, when most of the others have died. Write a diary for 3 days about what you see, think and feel.

© Hodder Murray 2006. Hodder Reading Project: Level 2–3

## Read Chapters 6 and 7

- Draw a diagram that shows how the plague was passed from person to person.

## After reading

- Use no more than 20 words to make notes about the history of the plague.

- Go to the library. In 15 minutes, see how much you can find out about life in 1386. Share your findings.

- Write a book review of *The Black Death* for other readers.

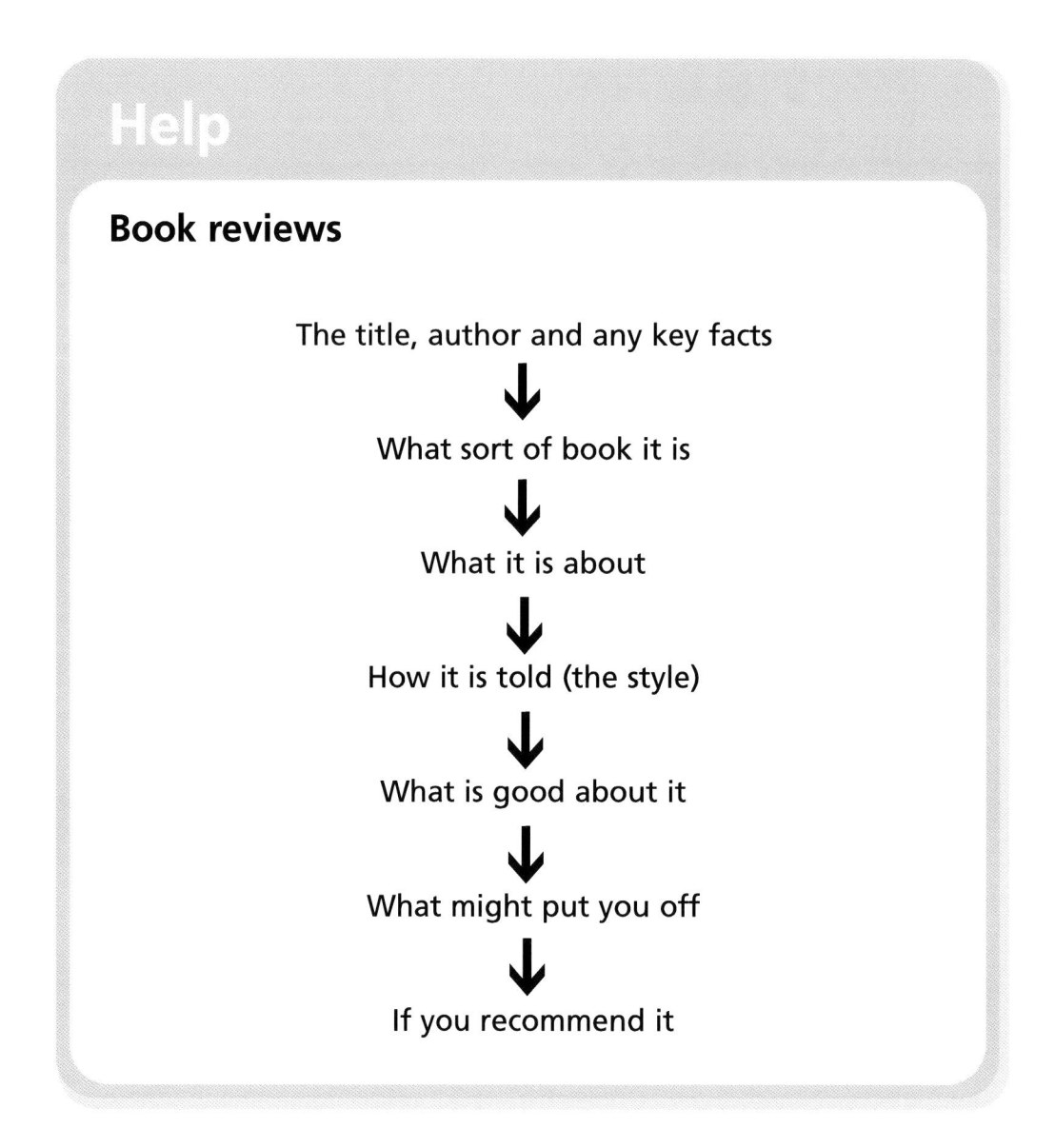

### Help

**Book reviews**

The title, author and any key facts
↓
What sort of book it is
↓
What it is about
↓
How it is told (the style)
↓
What is good about it
↓
What might put you off
↓
If you recommend it

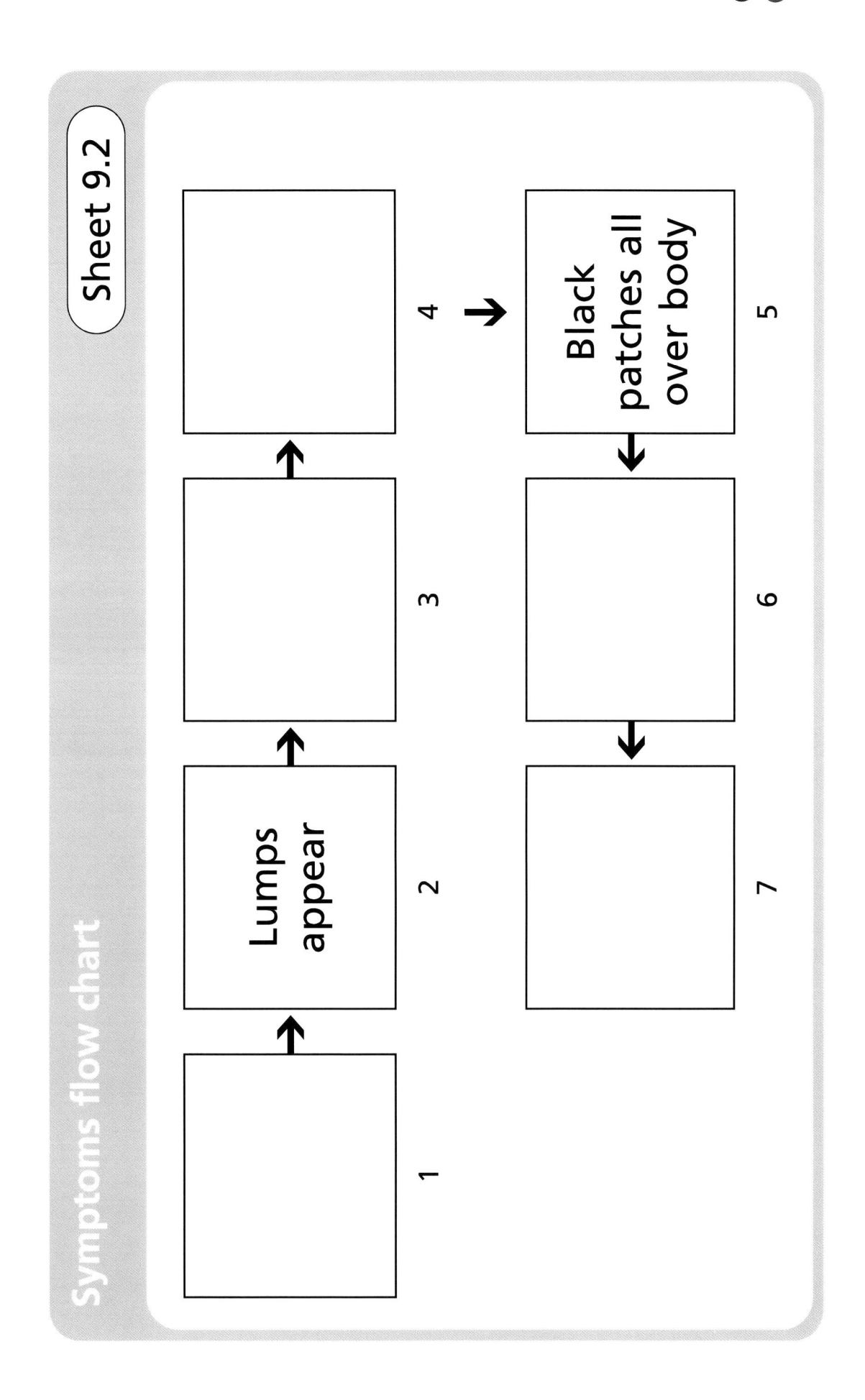

# Level 3: The Black Death

## Sheet 9.2
### Symptoms flow chart

| 1 | 2 | 3 | 4 | 5 |
|---|---|---|---|---|
|   | Lumps appear |   |   | Black patches all over body |

1 → 2 (Lumps appear) → 3 → 4 → 5 (Black patches all over body) → 6 → 7

© Hodder Murray 2006. Hodder Reading Project: Level 2–3

**HRP Teacher's Resource: Level 2 → 3**

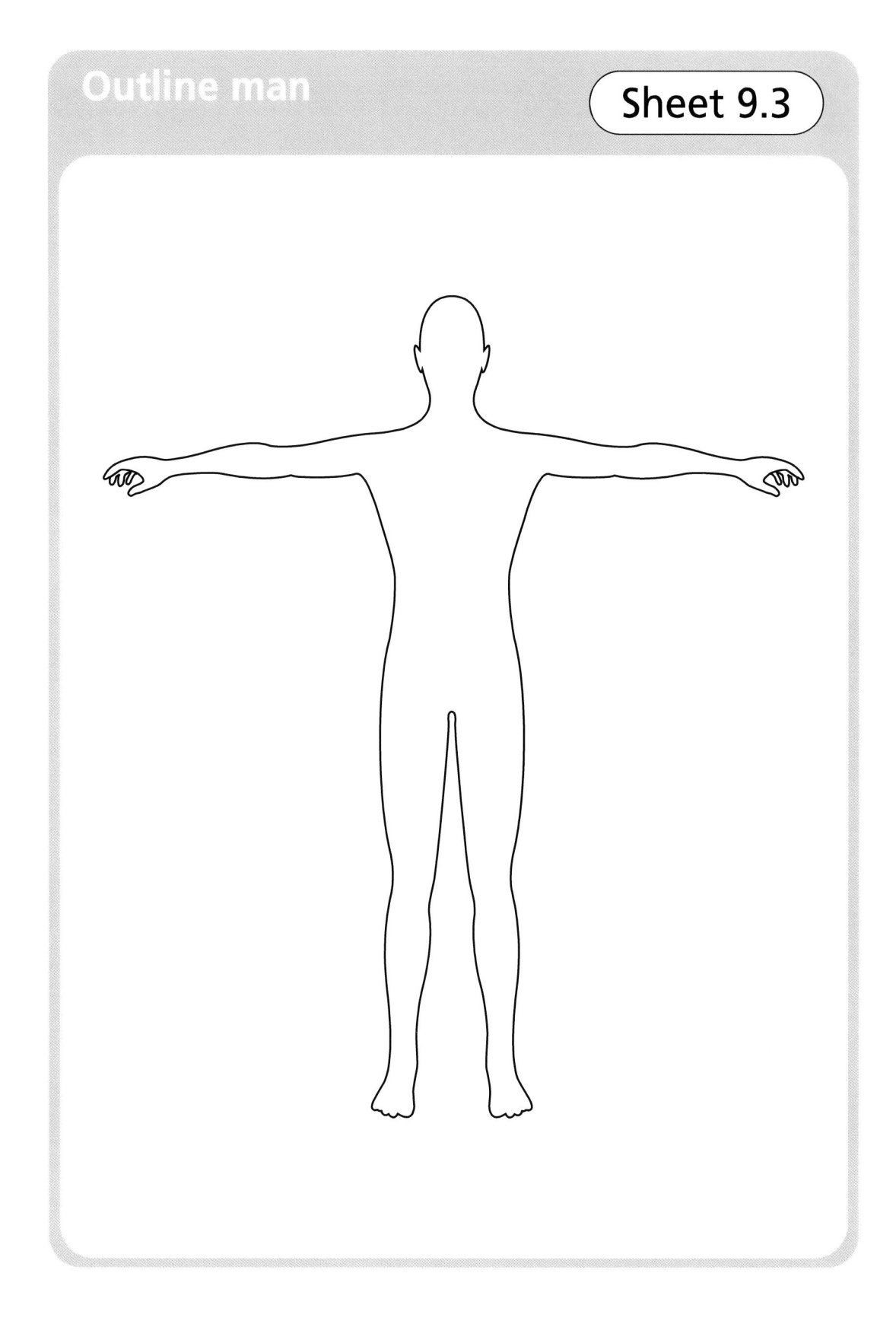

## Outline man

Sheet 9.3

**Level 3: You won't believe this but...**

## 10 You won't believe this but... by John Townsend

### Synopsis

The book contains an entertaining anthology of outrageous stories. Many are authenticated, but nonetheless bizarre.

### This reading book follows up these masterclasses

- B4: Using your experience
- B5: Thinking aloud
- B6: Reading like a detective
- C8: Working out words you don't know
- E15: Answering test questions

### You will need

- Sheet 10.1: Reading instructions (pp.96–97)

### Extension teaching points

- Sharing similar stories, e.g. from newspapers, family anecdote
- How stories are inflated as they pass from person to person
- The oral network – gossip, opinion, rumour, anecdote, etc.

**HRP Teacher's Resource: Level 2 → 3**

## You won't believe this but...
### Reading instructions

**Sheet 10.1**

## Read Chapter 1

- Can you remember any stories which were just too odd to believe?

## Read Chapter 2: Out of the Blue

- How do you explain things that fall out of the sky? Where can they have come from?

- There is a saying, 'It's raining cats and dogs'. Maybe it is true and not just a figure of speech! What other figures of speech are there for saying 'It's raining'?

## Read Chapter 3: Fishy Tales

- Do you believe these stories, and why? What are the signs that make you think a story really did happen?

- Fish are often linked to lies, e.g. 'A fishy story'. Can you think of any sayings that use fish? Why do fish have such a bad name?

- Do you know any other odd stories about fish?

## Read Chapter 4: Animal Antics

- A punchline is a last line that rounds off a joke and gets a laugh. These stories have punchlines. Spot the punchlines and say how each one packs a punch.

## Read Chapter 5: That was Close

- What is *A & E* (page 13)? Can you work it out?

- What is the medical term for *windpipe* (page 14)?

- What is a *baton* (page 14)? Can you work it out?

- The titles of some of the stories are jokes. Can you explain why?

© Hodder Murray 2006. Hodder Reading Project: Level 2–3

## Read Chapter 6: Nurse ... Help!

- Do you know any weird medical stories?

- What is the worst illness or accident you have ever had? Tell other people about it to amaze them. What do you do to make your story amazing?

## Read Chapter 7: What a Way to Go

- What do all the endings have in common?

- How likely is it that these are true stories? What clues are there that they are true? Are there any clues that they are false?

## Read Chapter 8: Almost the End

- There have always been strange stories about death. Do you know any?

- Why are there so many stories told about death? What is the appeal?

HRP Teacher's Resource: Level 2 → 3

## 11 Mini-sagas edited by Sue Hackman

### Synopsis

The book contains an anthology of high-impact stories produced during the *Daily Telegraph*'s mini-saga competition. Readers were invited to compose very short stories that were exactly 50 words in length.

### This reading book follows up these masterclasses

- A1: Seeing what you read
- A2: What next?
- A3: Feeling it
- B4: Using your experience
- B5: Thinking aloud
- B6: Reading like a detective
- E15: Answering test questions

### You will need

- Sheet 11.1: Reading instructions (pp.99–100)

### Extension teaching points

- Further mini-sagas to read in the books of published entries
- Much scope to generate and display pupils' mini-sagas

Level 3: Mini-sagas

## Mini-sagas
Reading instructions

Sheet 11.1

## Read the first group of mini-sagas called *Cautionary tales* (pages 3–6)

- What is the warning in each mini-saga?

- What do you think happens after the end of each mini-saga?

## Read the second group of mini-sagas called *Fantasy* (pages 7–11)

- Draw the alien in 'For Frank'.

- Who is *he* and who is *she* in 'Happily ever after'?

- Rewrite the ending of 'Time warp'. Keep the words up to *warily*, but write 22 new words after it.

- How does the writer make time stop in 'At noon'?

## Read the next pair of mini-sagas in *Oops!* (pages 12–14)

- Explain the mistakes.

- What do you think happens next?

- Give 2 reasons why mini-sagas often stop at the crisis point.

## Read the mini-sagas called *Riddles* (pages 15–18)

- Who are the son and the dad in 'Homecoming'? What do the nails and the kiss refer to?

- 'Life and numbers' is about the growth of a family over time. Can you explain what happens?

- There is no monkey in the last mini-saga. Can you explain it?

© Hodder Murray 2006. Hodder Reading Project: Level 2–3

## Read the mini-sagas called *Dreams come true* (pages 19–21)

- Change the title of 'A dream in an orphanage' to give it a completely different meaning.

- In 'To live again', what can you work out about the background of the family? How much time has passed?

## Read the last set of mini-sagas in *Sting in the tail* (pages 22–25)

- Look at the title and the last line of 'Pain in a bottle'. What has the victim done with his feelings?

- What is the daughter worried about in the last line of 'The death touch'?

- What are you listening to in 'Writing a mini-saga'?

## After reading

- Try writing a mini-saga. Remember: you have just 50 words, plus a title.

Level 3: The Red Fox

## 12 The Red Fox by Peter Leigh

### Synopsis

**Chapter 1:** Jo and Matt are intrigued by a document found during a survey of the derelict local Old Manor House.

**Chapter 2:** Jo and Matt study the document to make sense of the old language used in it. They discover clues about a hidden treasure.

**Chapter 3:** Jo and Matt search the internet for further information about the Red Fox. They discover some useful background information about their local history.

**Chapter 4:** Jo and Matt break into the derelict Old Manor House to seek the treasure, but at first they are unable to locate it. Then Jo suddenly sees the trail of clues hinted at in the document. They begin to follow them closer to the treasure.

**Chapter 5:** The trail leads to a secret underground chamber. Nervously, the pair lower themselves down into the darkness.

**Chapter 6:** As Jo and Matt look around the chamber, they hear footsteps approaching. Terrified, they cling together until the steps stop above their heads. They hear a voice call their names.

**Chapter 7:** Matt's dad has found them. They are hauled out and tell him everything. The 'treasure' is revealed and the mystery is solved.

### This reading book follows up these masterclasses

- A1: Seeing what you read
- A2: What next?
- A3: Feeling it
- B6: Reading like a detective
- C7: Sounding out words you don't know
- C8: Working out words you don't know
- C9: Reading longer sentences
- D10: Finding information
- E15: Answering test questions

### You will need

- Sheet 12.1: Reading instructions (pp.102–104)
- Sheet 12.2: Front page newspaper story (p.105)

**HRP Teacher's Resource: Level 2 → 3**

## The Red Fox
Reading instructions

Sheet 12.1

**You will need:**
Sheet 12.2: Front page newspaper story

## Before reading

- Discuss what you know about local history.
- Are there very old places near you?
- Do local place names tell you anything about the past in your area?

## Read Chapter 1

- How old are Matt and Jo, and how do you know?
- Work out the meaning of these words. Use clues in the text and clues in the words themselves:
  - ▶ *barbed* (page 3)
  - ▶ *surveyor* (page 4)
  - ▶ *fragile* (page 6)
- What do you think will happen in the story?

## Read Chapter 2

- Before there were dictionaries, people made up spellings. How did they do this?
- Why do you think people agreed to stick to the spellings listed in the dictionary?
- How do Matt and Jo work out what the letter says?
- What do you now think will happen in the story?

# Read Chapter 3

- Look up the history of your home-town on the web.
- What helps and what makes it hard to find information?
- Write tips for people using the web for research.

# Read Chapter 4

- The Old Manor is a scary place. Find all the words that tell you it is a scary and dangerous place.
- Draw a map or floor plan of the house and the path that Matt and Jo follow.
- Explain the following expressions:
  - *the windows were long gone* (page 20)
  - *doorways leading off it* (page 30)
  - *pick up the trail again* (page 31)
- What do you now think will happen in the story?

# Read Chapter 5

- How does the writer try to scare you?
- Explain the following expressions:
  - *a dead-end* (page 32)
  - *a dead thud* (page 33)
  - *trap-door* (page 35)

**HRP Teacher's Resource: Level 2→3**

## Read Chapter 6

- Draw the treasure room.

- What do you think the treasure is?

- The paragraph starting *And she didn't* (page 39) tells you what is going on in Jo's mind. How do you know?

- The sentences in that paragraph are long and broken up. How did you go about reading them?

- What do you now think will happen in the story?

## Read Chapter 7

- How close were you to guessing how the story would go?

## After reading

- Write the directions to get to the treasure room. Use words only.

- Write a front page story for the local newspaper about Matt and Jo finding the treasure. Use Sheet 12.2.

Level 3: The Red Fox

**Front page newspaper story**

Sheet 12.2

# Foxton News